Pueblo Indian Folk-Stories

THE BOY IN THE HOUSE OF THE TRUES. (SEE PAGE 115.)

PUEBLO INDIAN FOLK-STORIES

BY
CHARLES F. LUMMIS

Introduction to the Bison Book Edition
by Robert F. Gish

University of Nebraska Press
Lincoln and London

Introduction copyright © 1992 by the University of Nebraska Press
Manufactured in the United States of America

First Bison Book printing: 1992
Most recent printing indicated by the last digit below:
10   9   8   7   6   5   4   3   2   1

Library of Congress Cataloging-in-Publication Data
Lummis, Charles Fletcher, 1859–1928.
Pueblo Indian folk-stories / by Charles F. Lummis: introduction to the
Bison Book edition by Robert F. Gish.
p.   cm.
Previously published: New York: Century Co., 1910.
Includes bibliographical references.
ISBN 0-8032-7938-8 (pbk.)
1. Pueblo Indians—Legends. I. Title.
E99.P9L96   1992
398.2'08997—dc20   91-40614
CIP

Originally published as *The Man Who Married the Moon* in 1894 by the
Century Company, New York. This Bison Book is a reprint of the 1910
edition, which was expanded and retitled *Pueblo Indian Folk-Stories*.

♾

CONTENTS

LIST OF ILLUSTRATIONS

ix

These illustrations are from drawings by George Wharton Edwards,
after photographs by the author.

INTRODUCTION
by Robert F. Gish

Charles F. Lummis's *Pueblo Indian Folk-Stories* is a book worthy of reintroduction. First published as *The Man Who Married the Moon and Other Pueblo Indian Folk-Stories* in 1894 and again sixteen years later under the title of *Pueblo Indian Folk-Stories*, Lummis's narrations of Isleta myths allow readers crucial insight into Pueblo cultures and into Lummis's own encounters with them as a major nineteenth-century Anglo adventurer and writer in the American West.[1] Now, nearly a century later, this Bison reprint commemorates both the Pueblo peoples whose myths and stories Lummis sought to perpetuate and Lummis's own love for the region of the West that he took credit for naming "the Southwest."[2]

In the 1990s, as centennial exhibitions of Lummis's first "tramp across the continent" and personal "discovery" of the Southwest are staged, and the quincentenary of Columbus's "discovery" of America and its aboriginal inhabitants is both celebrated and condemned, it is especially appropriate to reissue *Pueblo Indian Folk-Stories*.[3]

Certainly Lummis was not Columbus. But in addition to characterizing himself as a "New Mexico David," he also thought fondly of the Spanish conquest of the New World, and particularly of Nueva Granada (the earlier designation of "the Southwest"). It is not surprising, then, to hear and take note of various Pueblo storytellers in *Pueblo Indian Folk-Stories* address Lummis as "Don Carlos," and for him to editorialize on the rightness of early Spanish dominion of the region.[4]

The Southwest and particularly New Mexico, true to its slogan as a land of enchantment, always enchanted Lummis, invigorated him, healed him, and became part of his own life myth. In *Pueblo Indian Folk-Stories* these enchantments come vividly to life in a collection of thirty-two myths (folk stories) that center around the Pueblo of Isleta, one of then about twenty occupied pueblos along or near the Rio Grande. Other pueblos, particularly the Keres (Queres) pueblos of Laguna and Acoma (some fifty or so miles to the west), come into play in the book, as does Lummis's autobiography. Through editorial commentary and a kind of "Pueblo-deco" point of view, Lummis dramatizes his friendships and fascinations with the Isletans who tell him these myths, what he calls "folk stories," adapting and retelling them for a wider, presumably eastern Anglo audience.

In his original introduction to *Pueblo Indian Folk-Stories* Lummis equates "myth" with "fairy stories," with oral traditions that date back to the "childhood of the human race" (p. 1). In seeing Pueblo myth as fairy or folk stories Lummis suggests a certain juvenile quality of his own narrative adaptations. They are wisdom stories that explain ageless truths about the mysterious, interconnecting ways of humans, animals, and gods. Their "juvenile" quality is not so much substantive as it is descriptive of the dramatized audience of children seated at the feet of tribal elders.

Certainly Lummis's attitude toward the Isletans as "child-like" should not be misinterpreted as paternalistic, patronizing, or disrespectful. Although certain present-day readers might place a political spin on these stories and see them as a bit condescending in overall narrative tone and feeling, Lummis was decidedly much ahead of other Anglo-Americans in his attitude toward Native Americans. Moreover, he clearly intended *Pueblo Indian Folk-Stories* as a tribute to Isleta and to Native American culture generally. In addition to the respect shown them in his writings, Lummis's legacy of the Southwest Museum near his eccentric rock-constructed residence, "El Alisal," in east Los Angeles offers further proof of his sustained respect for Native Americans and the sense of curiosity he felt about them and identification he felt with them.[5]

In an attempt to unify his collection of disparate stories, Lummis, from story to story, identifies his Isleta mythtellers as essentially seven elders who, seated around a winter fire at the pueblo or camped in the nearby Manzano Mountains, are variously introduced as Lorenso, Desiderio, Diego, Antonio, Felipe, Vitorino, Ysidro, and Anastacio. The respective narrators fuse into composites, however, evoking a kind of Pueblo chorus attempting to justify why things are so, and how they came to be. Adding to this chorus, Lummis is an ever-present intrusive narrator himself, intimately involved in listening and in telling and retelling.

If he favors any of his narrators, it is Desiderio—clearly his primary informant among not just the seven narrators but the 1,200 or so inhabitants of Isleta when Lummis lived there from 1888 to 1892. For instance, in a frightening fantasy about baby-eating ogres, "The Hungry Grandfathers," Lummis's digressive frame narration soon overtakes the story of the ogres and turns upon Desiderio's discovery of one of the chimneys to the home of the ogres on Tomé Hill, located near a neighboring village north of Isleta. Of his friend and informant, Desiderio Peralta, who is also one of the first-heard narrators in the collection, Lummis says, "[He] could have furnished an army of old men with wrinkles!" (p. 219). Ideal readers will allow Lummis literary license in such attempts at humanizing presumed exotic and alien individuals, and attempts that unintentionally promulgate "according to an old Indian" stereotypes.

Aside from his narrative attempts to bring greater unity to the stories, a great many of them do reflect the ties of Isleta to Acoma and especially to Laguna Pueblo. This is no deterrent to the overall unified effect of the thirty-two stories, for many of them are thematically interconnected. The Laguna-Isleta kinship is of considerable historical significance to the ritual and literary traditions of the Isletans, and Lummis goes to some lengths to differentiate the

Keres myths (Acoma and Laguna) from Tiwa myths (Isleta, Sandia, Picuris, Taos, and other older Tiguex, Tanoan Pueblos). Moreover, he also attempts to separate post-Spanish myths, especially those that allude to horses or burros (animals introduced by the Spanish), from Isleta myths.

Pueblo Indian Folk-Stories, in its attempts at shaping and unifying Isleta and Laguna Pueblo myth in a single volume, helps readers understand why the Pueblo culture of the Rio Grande is so wonderfully complex. This complexity is enhanced by its ever-changing parade of interpreters and their respective attitudes and assumptions. In understanding Lummis's versions of more ancient stories, it is important to know that following religious splits at Laguna in 1881 many Laguna dissidents traveled to Isleta, where they were welcomed, and influenced Isleta rituals with Laguna kachina masks and other anthropomorphic myths and stories.[6]

Lummis, true to the history of both Isleta and Laguna, incorporates many myths that reflect these migrations and assimilations. In this context readers should note "The Moki Boy and the Eagle," "The North Wind and the South Wind," "The Sobbing Pine," "The Queres Diana," "A Pueblo Bluebeard," and "The Hero Twins." "The Drowning of Pecos" involves an even more convoluted retelling of Pecos Pueblo myth, heard in the pueblo of Jemez and retold to Lummis by an Isletan. It is because of such pan-pueblo stories in *Pueblo Indian Folk-Stories* that Lummis's insights into the larger Pueblo culture should be appreciated.

Most of the stories in the collection, Lummis says, were told to him in Spanish and many do reflect the three and a half centuries through which Isleta was influenced by Spanish dominion, especially Catholicism and the Spanish language.[7] *Pueblo Indian Folk-Stories*, in its English retelling of Spanish accounts of Tiwa and Keres myth, affords intriguing linguistic lessons that not only enhance "local color" but go beyond it to help capture the many cultural laminations of the region. Lummis concedes much linguistic difficulty of Pueblo languages (*e.g.*, Zuñi, Keresan, and Kiowa-

Tanoan, which includes Tiwa). And it is important when reading the stories to note that such translations as exist in Lummis's retellings and in his narrator's Spanish accounts are as much attributable to his and the Isletan's fluency in Spanish and English as to their mutual fluency in Tiwa. Lummis, however, in his performance and presence as narrator, translator, linguist, artist, and anthropologist, is convincing in his insistence that he strives for essences, for the spirit of the stories rather than the letter.

In his translations and in his arrangements of the stories and the myths embodied in them, Lummis presents Isleta myths and rituals as examples of wisdom and initiation narratives common to Pueblo oral tradition. Here are stories, we are to accept (albeit in a slightly less a innocent way than the children listening to them in the narrative formulations) that tell what happens when the strictures of the "Trues," the powerful Isletan deities, are violated. Ramon, Benito, Fat Juan (Juan Bischocho), and Tomas (as well as Lummis and the non-Indian reader along with him), are just a few of the innocents seated at the feet of the seven "viejos" (old ones) who serve up, usually through the offerings of cigarette smoke, special words to justify the verities of Isleta tradition. In a world of old men and boys the only contemporary Isleta woman is one Grandmother Reyes, whose female task it is, in "The Coyote and the Bear," to unroll the mattresses on the floor when the night's storytelling is over. As a *vecino* or neighbor, Lummis stresses that he is privileged to sit by the winter fires smoldering in sympathy with the word-ways which mark not only these long nights of the book's present but the cyclical echoes of more ancient ones.

In the account of "The Brave Bobtails," a delightful "mythic" explanation of how the bear and the badger came to have short tails when they attempted to rescue a mighty Ute hunter, Lummis observes, "It has always seemed to me that the boy who always wants to know 'why?' has a better time of it among my Indian friends than anywhere else. For there is always sure to be a why, and an interesting one—which is much more satisfactory than only learning that 'it's bedtime now,' or that 'I'm busy'" (p. 177). Notwithstanding the reductive cross-cultural assumptions of such an endorsement, suffering to help a friend, although it means losing a tail, is decidedly an honorable act—a small price to pay.

The "brown story-tellers," as Lummis calls them, explain the "whys" of many things: why coyotes are always at war with crows and blackbirds, woodpeckers and bears; how rattlesnakes came to have rattles and poison while certain other snakes are harmless; why before and during the scalp dance there should be no thoughts of love; why arrow heads are called "thunder knives." Each of these Tiwa stories builds to "folk" explanations that find their truth in their beauty and invention as well as in their tradition.

Isleta as a place in these tales extends much beyond the Pueblo as center, into the Manzano and Sandia mountains to the east, and beyond them to the *Llano Estacado,* the staked plains known to the Pueblos much before these vast grass lands were marked by the Spanish. The dark, volcanic loomings to Tomé Hill, the plateau known as the Black Mesa that marks the southern boundary of the present Isleta reservation, the salt lakes in the southern Manzanos, the villages of Mesita and Las Padillas—all of these special and community-defining landmarks are given a special animism throughout. Personification of the moon and the sun, of stars and planets, of plants and crops (especially corn), of rocks, trees, and bushes, mesas and mountains, rivers and winds, landforms and elements, make for magical and compelling adventures; momentous odysseys of birth and death, of creation and destruction, trickery and gullibility, falseness and fakery deservedly undone.

"The Man Who Married the Moon," the original titular story of the collection is an excellent instance of Lummis's predictions and his techniques as an adapter of Isleta myth. Several sequels of this story are interpolated throughout the other stories, amplifying this central account of one of Isleta's most charismatic and potent heroes. He is Nah-chu-ru-chu, a young weaver, wise beyond his years in medicine and healing. In his life, too, as in his art and in

Lummis's, pattern and color and right action take the shape and the goodness of story. The identity of his bride and how he came to choose her take on much consequence for the entire population in those very early days of the Pueblo.

Nah-chu-ru-chu, along with other heroes such as Antelope Boy, Corn Stalk Boy, and the Hero Twins operate in a world where extreme remedies prevail. Nah-chu-ru-chu's time and world are long ago near Eagle-Feather Mountain in the Place of the Red Earth. In "The First of the Rattle Snakes" he suffers betrayal and transformation but ultimately punishes treachery and helps his people. The means by which he does so are dramatic; no half-way measures will work.

Besides cosmic, elemental, topographical, horticultural, and regional presences, there is much powerful fabulation in these stories. As for the bestiary represented here, animals take on significant roles both as characters and as exemplars much beyond any fatuous cartoons for children. Here we meet Eagle, Hawk, Beaver, Mole, Mouse, Coyote, Badger, Bear, Rabbit, Turkey Buzzard, Ant, Horned Toad, and Deer. All such creatures take on the larger designations of general human urgency, of life force and survival, of struggles between good and evil.

Taken individually and as a whole, *Pueblo Indian Folk-Stories* may be regarded as accountings of the continuing struggles for reconciliation between humans, with the gods, and with the natural world—the striving after some sense of wholeness and harmony. Lummis's Tee-wahn versions of Tiwa folk stories, like other Pueblo myths, offer words of warning and defeat, reaffirmation and triumph. These are stories not just by which the Isletans lived and continue to live, but a lesson and benediction, proof once again of the procreative power of story, itself a mythic inspiration. For this we owe Lummis our appreciation. Throughout the pages of *Pueblo Indian Folk-Stories* we can sense his own self-proclaimed but deserved pride in sharing his continuing legacy of "the Southwest" as he knew it and rendered it. His Southwest was a place, both permanent and changing, which he allows us at least partially to see through these nineteenth-century recountings of Isleta Pueblo. But who really was this man, and how did he come to write this book and to deserve remembering?

Whoever Lummis was before he went to his Southwest, and particularly New Mexico, he was never the same after "discovery." As it did D. H. Lawrence and so many others over the centuries, New Mexico remade Lummis and became—as place, as people, and as idea—his life myth. Even in a book of myths that center around Isleta Pueblo, Lummis's autobiography is obvious, for his prominence as narrator is everywhere dramatized: through editorializing, anecdote, intrusive aside. *Pueblo Indian Folk-Stories* is directly tied to perhaps the most important period of his life, from 1888 to 1892, when Lummis actually took up residence at Isleta. It was a familiar transition in United States history and story: an easterner is transformed by the American West—and reciprocally transforms it in words.

Lummis was forever fascinated with words, with writing—a fascination waiting to be kindled by the vistas and spaces, the lives and landscapes of the Southwest. In Lynn, Massachusetts, as a boy, and later at Harvard University, indications were that writing would help direct his life's calling and the calling of the West. During summers in college he worked as a printer. After his marriage to Dorothea Roads and their move to Ohio, he worked as editor of the *Scioto Gazette* in Chillicothe. By arrangement with the *Los Angeles Times*, he contracted to submit weekly articles about a long sojourn by foot from Ohio to California. Once his trek had taken him to California, he worked as editor for the *Times* and later covered the Apache wars in Arizona.

In 1888, due to overwork and pressures of city life, he suffered the first of several strokes, which partially paralyzed his left arm, affected his gait and his speech and helped him decide to return to New Mexico—first to San Mateo, near Grants, where he stayed again with Amado Chaves, a latter-day Spanish aristocrat and New Mexico territorial attorney and politician whom Lummis had met earlier on his three-thousand-mile "tramp across the continent." Mutual accounts of their friendship confirm that their meeting helped solidify Lummis's claim to New Mexico citizenship, even when living in California. It was a friendship that, after his stroke, drew him back for a recuperative stay much longer than the initial week's visit in 1884. Most importantly, it was a friendship that positioned him for his move to Isleta and the recording of the myths in *Pueblo Indian Folk-Stories*.

It was, according to Chaves's account, Lummis's photographs of secret Penitente crucifixion rituals near San Mateo, and the printing of those pictures in *Scribner's Magazine*, that led to numerous threats to his life and culminated in an attempted ambush outside his Isleta house in February 1889. As printed in Lummis's *Land of Poco Tiempo* (1893), those photographs and their violation of sect taboo were the probable cause of the ambush and near-murder, and not Lummis's involvement in a range war as is also speculated. Whatever the causes of such danger and intrigue, Lummis's years at Isleta provided the stuff of his own life myth as well as the Pueblo folk stories.[8]

At Isleta, Lummis was drawn back into the mythic Native American and Spanish past. He had visited the pueblo on his original westering trip and had described his reactions to the ceremony of the "Fiesta De Los Muertos" (the Celebration of the Day of the Dead) in *A Tramp across the Continent*. In taking up residence there in a house rented from Maria Garcia Chihuihui, the wife of Antonio Jojola, Lummis sought to explore further the culture and myths of this particular Tiwa branch of Pueblo culture.[9] He carried out his explorations at the pueblo in part through what today can only be thought of as wondrous Dallmeyer five-by-eight-inch photographs and by listening to and composing these "Indian fairy stories or folk stories," as he designated them. As the dedication to the book reveals, he created a lasting autobiographical bond to Isleta through meeting Eve Douglas there: "To the fairy tale that came true in the Home of the Tee-wahn, my wife and child."

During his stay at Isleta he divorced Dorothea Roads and married Eve Douglas, his neighbor and the sister-in-law of an Isleta trader.[10] His new wife gave birth to their first child, an event that occasioned a report by Lummis on his relations with the Isletans.[11] The Isletans, Lummis asserted, thought of him as a wizard and, if not a witch, then at least bewitched. Although the natural cause of his paralysis and illness was a stroke, the Isletans, he said, believed that he should directly confront the witch who had cast a spell on him. His eventual recovery—due to "a powerful constitution and an out-door life"—convinced his Pueblo neighbors that he had paid other witches to cure him.[12] His exposure to such attitudes helps explain the high incidence of stories dealing with bewitchment in *Pueblo Indian Folk-Stories*.[13]

Lummis's degree of acceptance into Pueblo inner circles is, as dramatized in the stories, quite extraordinary and perpetuates his own life myth as an archetypal Anglo-American initiate into Native American culture, a familiar myth in western literature. He portrays himself, too, through his footnotes and refinements of remote and subtle Pueblo meanings, as an anthropologist hero in something of the same outline as his friend and contemporary, Adolph Bandelier. We are led to believe that Lummis is engaging in serious field work in addition to producing literary entertainments.

Lummis's narrative personae, as adventurer, writer, anthropologist, and friend are not wholly imaginary ones. They were perpetuated in both his life and his writings. Lummis's life myth merging with Isleta myth is obvious from the very first story, "The Antelope Boy," when as the narrative begins, he identifies himself as benefactor: "[Lorenso] pauses only to make a cigarette from the material in my pouch (they call me 'Por todos,' because I have tobacco for all".[14] Today his pueblo folk stories extend his benevolence.

The history of Isleta Pueblo, its people, and its location in the Southwest of map and mind is a much larger story and process than

Lummis's years of convergence with it. Isleta, the "island" pueblo, is rich in comparative Native American/Hispanic/Anglo cultures. Located twelve miles south of Albuquerque, Isleta, among all the pueblos, has its own special historical and cultural fascinations, in part because of its proximity to one of the largest southwestern cities. Furthermore, Isleta's location on the north-south axis of Rio Grande migrations positions it at the historical crossroads of southwestern exploration and settlement—from much before the coming of the Conquistadors, through the frontier and railroad periods, through the atomic age and into the space and high-tech computer eras of the twentieth century.

It is by virtue of its location on a lava mesa or promontory which was long ago an island in the Rio Grande that Isleta takes its Spanish name or variously that of San Agostín, or St. Augustine, the name, too, of its legendary Catholic church. The Pueblo's Tiwa name is Shiw'iba or, as Lummis designates it, Shee-eh-whib-bak—that is, "knife laid on the ground to play *whib*," a name coined from a foot race where runners carry a stick with their toes, and reminiscent of the fleet-footed contests that pervade the myths in *Pueblo Indian Folk-Stories*. Among the stories dealing with tricks and rigged races between animals, men, and gods, readers will find "The Race of the Tails" and "The Antelope Boy" of interest.

As described by Lummis in his introductory "Brown Story Tellers" Isleta at the time of his residence there was an idyllic place. It was "nearly surrounded by fertile vineyards, orchards of peaches, apricots, apples, cherries, plums, pears, and quince, and fields of corn, wheat, beans, and peppers, all owned by my dusky neighbors." He goes on to describe the Isletans as physically short and stout with "magnificent depth and breadth of chest, and a beautifully confident poise of the head" (p. 4). The actual census of 1890 reported the population of Isleta as 1,059. A century later, Isleta, as one of the region's largest still inhabited pueblos, is home for approximately three thousand people, many of whom work in the adjacent towns of Los Lunas, Belen, and Albuquerque. The Isleta Reservation, geographically, extends from the Manzano Mountains to the east, to the Rio Puerco to the west, and encompasses 209,891 acres.[15]

Much of Isleta and Pueblo history involves the explorations and colonization of Spain in the Southwest. Consistent with his efforts to preserve California's Spanish missions, Lummis is, throughout *Pueblo Indian Folk-Stories*, in sympathy with Spanish dominion over the Pueblos. He does not question the assumptions of Spanish conquest. Certainly the anger and hostility of the larger Pueblo revolt of 1680, which so drastically undercuts the Spanish phase of Pueblo involvement is nowhere seen in *Pueblo Indian Folk-Stories*. In part this is explainable by Lummis's intent to "transcribe" and reshape myths and stories intended, at a fundamental level, for the instruction and edification of youths. It is also explainable in that, for reasons not fully understood by historians, Isleta did not participate in the original massacre of the Pueblo Revolt. The Spanish did attack Isleta, burn the pueblo, and take over five hundred captives. And during the revolt the move to Isleta of over a thousand settlers from the town of Bernalillo solidified Spanish control so that when Governor Antonio de Otermín and other refugees from Santa Fe reached Isleta they found the few Isletans who remained increasingly hostile. A small number of the Isletans were resettled farther south, near El Paso, at what came to be called Ysleta del Sur.[16]

Spanish records, especially the Benavides Memorial published in Madrid in 1630, establish that the mission at Isleta was flourishing as early as 1629, having been established, in Catholic perception, in 1612 by Friar Juan de Salas. Readers interested in tracing aspects of Spanish influence in the stories Lummis narrates should take note, too, of the assumptions about witchcraft throughout. Although such themes are closely tied to superstition and traditional native religions, they also carry the colorizations of Spanish colonization and religious conversion and heresy. Such stories include "The Man Who Wouldn't Keep Sunday." *Pueblo Indian Folk-*

Stories thus suggests that whether interpreted by Lummis or others, pure Pueblo myth is not easy to isolate, given the tremendous changes which Spanish Catholicism infused into Native American comprehension of and accountability for deity and morality.

The Pueblo people afford an amazing example of cultural preservation and of assimilation and adaptation to other controlling cultures, be they Spanish, Mexican, or American. And in *Pueblo Indian Folk-Stories* Lummis serves up only versions of whatever truths these stories attempt to represent. In his original introduction to the book he acknowledges that

> Isletan secret inner religion is one of the most complicated systems on earth. Besides the highest deities, all the forces of nature, all animals, as well as many things that are inanimate, are invested by them with supernatural powers. They do not worship idols, but images and tokens of unseen powers. . . . They do nothing without some reason, generally a religious one, and whatever they observe they can explain in their own superstitious way. Every custom they have and every belief they own has a reason which to them is all-sufficient; and for each they have a story. There is no duty to which a Pueblo child is trained in which he has to be content with the bare command, 'Do thus'; for each he learns a fairy tale designed to explain how people first came to know that it was right to do thus. . . ."

Isleta culture and myth are merely part of larger Pueblo culture and myth and Lummis merely one interpreter of the traditional oral literature of the Pueblos. Current figures place the entire Pueblo population at about 36,000 people residing in eight northern pueblos and ten southern ones.[17] Keresan, Tanoan, and Zuñi are the major language groups. There are two dialects of the Tanoan language: Tiwi (which includes Isleta, Taos, Sandia, and Picuris) and Tewa (which includes San Juan, Santa Clara, San Ildefonso, Nambe, Tesuque, and Pojoaque). Such variety of language and dialect and the attendant variations of how oral traditions function in the respective societies illustrates how easy it is to oversimplify just what Lummis attempts in the stories reprinted here. As Spanish hegemony diminished, English replaced Spanish as a language of accommodation for the Pueblos. Revered communications still depend on tribal languages and "in the religious or classic languages, the vocabulary and terminology remain unchanged."[18] Lummis's oral retellings must essentially be seen as entertainments, themselves recast in the Spanish of an earlier century when Spanish influence was still compelling. Pueblo oral tradition and the myths and stories it imparts are, then, much more complex than Lummis's renderings, on first glance, might suggest. Among the more accessible books on Pueblo oral narrative performance, Dennis Tedlock's *Finding the Center*, also a Bison Book edition, helps demonstrate, in terms of Zuñi narrative poetry, just how simultaneously simple and involved (linguistically and culturally and aesthetically) Pueblo oral tradition actually is.

If one contrasts Tedlock's and other anthropologists' accounts of their laborious and fastidious field studies of Pueblo languages and cultures with Lummis's descriptions of his storytelling sessions with the Isletans, it soon becomes clear that he was more the artist-raconteur than the social scientist. He is, he himself stresses, not so much interested in the letter of these stories as in the spirit. A literal translation, he insisted at the beginning of the 1894 edition, would be "unintelligible to English readers" but he also insisted that he took no liberties "with the real meaning." The strength of his control of the original myths and, now in the retelling, of their English readers (listeners) is apparent. Contemporary readers who feel empowered with much more autonomy than Lummis anticipates will no doubt find ironies and distances (between Lummis and his personae and Isletan narrators; between author, and story, and reader) never dreamed of by Lummis's confident voice. Such methodology and result, we must acquiesce, offers us a result, say what you will about accuracy, we would not have otherwise. What Tedlock says about his own frustrations with the "truths" of translation may be applied to Lummis's stories and perhaps all stories as well: "nothing I could do would make [readers] experience these stories precisely as a Zuñi does. But there is no single, 'correct' picture of a given story even from one Zuñi to another."[19] It is, then, in keeping with much current literary theory and Pueblo oral tradition, no small thing to find our own truths in these stories in the same way that Lummis did and that countless Isletans did before him and with him. In a sense, the telling is all and it is enough.

Anthropologist have generally paid more attention to Isleta and to *Pueblo Indian Folk-Stories* than have literary critics. Few literary critics or authors, with the exception of Hamlin Garland, have been drawn to Isleta. It is their loss. Along with commentary by such notable anthropologists as Alfonso Ortiz, Florence Hawley Ellis, Elsie Clews Parsons, and Adolph Bandelier, Lummis's literary, stylized encapsulations of Isleta myth and legend, although not always seen as scientifically authoritative, nevertheless should continue to attract readers interested in him and in Pueblo culture. His first-hand look into the ultimately unfathomable mysteries of Isleta myth, into Isleta ritual as literature and literature as ritual, continues to fascinate "tourists" of a later century. In the special sense of the ebb and flow of historical process, the point then is not how scientifically accurate Lummis is in his recountings of Pueblo myth, but that at his particular point in time he chose to move to the pueblo and to become a mutual part of Isleta "legend." He carried through with the enterprise with much honesty, albeit the honesty of art.

Parsons records that when *Pueblo Indian Folk-Stories* came to the attention of certain Isleta leaders in 1927, some thirty-odd years after it was first published, the Pueblo council queried the possible informants and determined that the stories were "not very important" and were "mostly of Laguna [Pueblo], ... got by Lummis from one Patricio, now dead,"[20] In Parsons's account, however, it is clear that internal Pueblo politics and recriminations against an alleged tribal informant (Pablo Abeita) were overshadowing the actual and fictive "truths" of Lummis's stories. Any wider public revelation of traditional Pueblo belief is understandably discouraged and often, after the fact, defensively discounted.

All in all, what Lummis's first bit of bold tourism actually did was change his life and, in consequence, contribute to an attitude and set of assumptions much larger than Lummis both in its origin and in its final playing out—the romantic perception of the American Southwest as a sublime landscape with spectacular geographical and geological vistas, shapes, and spaces; an environment filled with wondrous flora and fauna; an exotic land peopled by dusky races of Indians and Mexicans with strange cultures and brave histories worthy of explanation, description, and interpretation. Certainly he was not the first curious Anglo-European tourist to traverse the American Southwest who regarded its inhabitants in need of explaining by "us"—that is, explanation of natives by non-natives to non-natives.

Although, in varying degrees, most Anglo-European westering shares similar stranger-in-a-strange-land attitudes, not all such travelers were similarly well-intentioned or motivated. The Conquistadors, of course, preceded Lummis and his turn-of-the-century kind—bringing with them somewhat different aims of gain and glory. So had the priestly orders who sought to "save" the "savages" they encountered. But whether motivated by curiosity or conquest, light-skinned "explorers" confronted dark-skinned "inhabitants"—alien forces in cultural and political contact, European exoticism transported to the new world.

Pueblo Indian Folk-Stories is part of that process. Even so, Lummis's Tee-wahn versions of Tiwa folk stories, like most myths, offer words and actions of fear and warning, of defeat and triumph, and of human affirmation. These are stories not just to which the Isletans listened, to which Lummis listened, but an inspiration to us all. They offer proof once again of the efficacy and healing power of stories as "word medicine."

We owe Lummis our thanks for *Pueblo Indian Folk-Stories* and for his other writings by which current talk about New History and New Ethnicity can be gauged. It is important to see Lummis's self-celebrations of "The Southwest" in even more crucial contexts of multi-racial and multi-cultural understanding—even more urgent means of understanding ourselves by understanding others. Lummis was one of the few Anglo-American writers to observe Isleta and comment on its positioning inside and outside of time, its ambivalently welcomed and resisted transitions into the twentieth century. Hamlin Garland also visited Isleta in 1895—a year after *Pueblo Indian Folk-Stories'* first publication. For Garland, Isleta remained a dream, a fantasy, born of his reading, "not of [his] actual living."²¹ Isleta, for Lummis, became its own kind of dream come true as seen both in his living there and the reading about it that *Pueblo Indian Folk-Stories* now again affords us.

NOTES

1. Charles F. Lummis, *The Man Who Married the Moon and Other Pueblo Indian Folk Stories* (New York: Century Co., 1894). Revised and enlarged as *Pueblo Indian Folk-Stories* (New York: Century Co., 1910).

2. "I was the first to apply . . . the generic christening by which it ['the million square miles which include New Mexico, Arizona, Southern California, and adjoining parts of Colorado, Utah, Texas, and Northern Mexico'] is now commonly known—THE SOUTHWEST," writes Lummis in *Mesa, Cañon and Pueblo* (New York: Century Co., 1925), p. vii. *Mesa* is a revision of Lummis's fourth book *Some Strange Corners of Our Country* (1892), and both books preview his interest in Pueblo culture as evidenced in *Pueblo Indian Folk-Stories*.

3. Lummis's career as writer, editor, photographer, amateur ethnologist, and tourist-adventurer, for all practical purposes, began in 1884 when, at the age of twenty-five, he decided to walk from Cincinnati, Ohio, to Los Angeles, California. Six months later, on February 1, 1885, he took a job as a city editor for the *Los Angeles Times*. The experiences of his westering

ostensibly provided the material for one of his earliest and best-known books, *A Tramp across the Continent* (1892) and gave rise to another of his claims: the coining of the slogan "See America First."

4. If Columbus is met today by Native Americans and New Historians with new realizations and regrets about the processes of domination then set into place, some of Lummis's self-claimed accomplishments must also be seen as contributing to Anglo-European attempts to recreate Native Americans in their own image, or as reflections of their own "white" images and imaginings. In the reporting and fabricating of encounters with the Pueblos and, certainly in the retellings, the "translations" of their own myths such as those narrated by Lummis's "Don Carlos" persona, Lummis also contributes to early versions of the "White Man's Indian." To see Lummis through present-day revisionist eyes as part of not just the historical processes and assumptions that Columbus helped set in motion but part of the often inane, curio-driven kitsch of once-authentic southwestern cities such as Santa Fe, is not to dismiss him nativistically as an egregious interloper, or a corrupter of once pristine indigenous cultures. But his interpretations of THE SOUTHWEST, *his* Southwest, were essentially oriented toward Anglo-American tourism and boosterism.

5. During his telling of one of the myths late in the volume, *i.e.,* "The Revenge of the Fawns," Lummis points explicitly to his own ill-founded fears and prejudices and the marvel of what brought him to Isleta and his enlightenment and revaluation of Anglo attitudes: "By this time, however, having lived long among the kindly Pueblos, I had shaken off the strange, ignorant prejudice against all that is unknown—which seems to be inborn in all of us—and wondered that I could ever have believed in that brutal maxim, worthy only of worse than savages, that 'A Good Indian is a dead Indian,' For Indians are men, after all and astonishingly like the rest of us when one really comes to know them" (p. 179). Although such a "confession" might sound condescending today, Lummis sought to enlighten his largely eastern, Anglo-American audience in ways that were quite in advance of their time. Native Americans, it must be remembered with dismay, were only first allowed to vote in the United States in 1924!

6. For a detailed account of Isleta prehistory and history in relation to

other pueblos, see Florence Hawley Ellis, "Isleta Pueblo," *Handbook of North American Indians: Southwest,* Vol. 9, ed. Alfonso Ortiz (Washington, D.C.: Smithsonian Institution, 1979), pp. 351–54. Ellis dates the Laguna-Isleta phase of acculturation as the last quarter of the nineteenth century and the Laguna split as one between progressive and conservative factions over the stresses of non-Indian contact.

7. Note, for example, the Spanish names of the narrators and Lummis's own personae of "Don Carlos," "Americano," and "Por todos."

8. Marc Simmons testifies that it was during Lummis's 1888 stay in the Chaves household that Lummis began, through the rigors of hunting and ranch chores, to recover from his stroke to the point that he began making excursions into the mesa wilderness, excavating Indian ruins, photographing the spectacular landscape, and generally attempting to "prove that he was greater than anything that could happen to him," Marc Simmons, *Two Southwesterns: Charles Lummis and Amado Chaves,* San Marcos Press, 1968), p. 15. For a detailed account of Lummis's photographic methods and techniques, including how Isleta water caused spotting on his prints, see Patrick T. Houlihan and Carolee Campbell, "Lummis as Photographer," *Charles F. Lummis: The Centennial Exhibition, Commemorating His Tramp across the Continent,* ed. Daniela P. Moneta (Los Angeles: Southwest Museum, 1985), pp. 21–34.

9. See Lummis, *Some Strange Corners of Our Country,* p. 256.

10. See Daniel P. Moneta, ed., *Charles F. Lummis: The Centennial Exhibition* (Los Angeles: Southwest Museum, 1985), p. 11. See Also, Robert E. Flemming, *Charles F. Lummis* (Boise, Id.: Western Writers Series, No. 50, 1981), p. 11.

11. Lummis, *Some Strange Corners of Our Country,* p. 257.

12. Lummis, *Some Strange Corners,* p. 74.

13. Elsie Clews Parsons, "The Pueblo of Isleta: A Definitive Report," *Indian Classics Series,* Vol. 1 (Albuquerque: University of Albuquerque, 1974), p. 207, reports that Lummis's Isleta name was PAXOLA or star and that he was well liked at the Pueblo.

14. For a number of years and especially now in the last decade of the twentieth century, Lummis's name and benevolence are most visibly and

(notwithstanding his many books), most lastingly present in the Highland Park area of Los Angeles. There, amid the Southern California ambiance of freeways, palm trees, and East L.A.'s predominantly Chicano population, are two special physical legacies: Lummis's home, *El Alisal*, and a few blocks away on a hill overlooking the Arroyo Seco locale of his abode, the Southwest Museum, formally opened to the public in 1914. *El Alisal*, named for a large native sycamore around which Lummis personally built his home out of the indigenous rocks and stones of the dry arroyo at the site, remains a testimonial to his indomitable and ever-resourceful southwestern spirit.

The Southwest Museum, as one of the earliest quality museums in the United States dedicated to preserving and exhibiting native cultures of the Americas, demonstrates in its own compelling, visual ways just why Lummis was so attracted to the Native American and Hispanic cultures and their encounters with each other in that historical period.

Looking at the exhibits of the Southwestern rooms of the Museum, or at Lummis's manuscripts collected there, his remarkable life as his own special kind of Southwestern discoverer, observer, reporter, and indeed, mythmaker, takes on special shape and meaning. It is a meaning made all the more notable for the five years he lived at Isleta. Lummis's role as benefactor is also noted in his lasting attempts to help restore and preserve the Spanish missions along California's El Camino Real.

15. See Anne M. Smith, *New Mexico Indians*, Museum of New Mexico Research Records, No. 1, p. 101.

16. See Ellis, p. 354.

17. See Joe S. Sando, *The Pueblo Indians* (San Francisco: Indian Historian Press, 1982), p. 239.

18. Sando, p. 5.

19. Dennis Tedlock, "Introduction," *Finding the Center: Narrative Poetry of the Zuñi Indians* (Lincoln: University of Nebraska Press, 1978), p. xxxi.

20. See Parsons, *The Pueblo of Isleta*, p. 207.

21. Hamlin Garland, "A Day at Isleta," *Hamlin Garland's Observations on the American Indian, 1895–1905*, Lonnie E. Underhill and Daniel F. Littlefield, Jr., eds. (Tucson: University of Arizona Press, 1976), p. 81.

THE BROWN STORY-TELLERS

I FANCY that if almost any of us were asked, "When did people begin to make fairy stories?" our first thought would be, "Why, of course, after mankind had become civilized, and had invented writing." But in truth the making of myths, which is no more than a dignified name for "fairy stories," dates back to the childhood of the human race.

Long before Cadmus invented letters (and I fear Cadmus himself was as much of a myth as was his dragon's-teeth harvest), long before there were true historians or poets, there were fairy stories and story-tellers. And to-day, if we would seek the place where fairy stories most flourish, we must go, not to the nations whose countless educated minds are now devoted to story-telling for the young, but to peoples who have no books, no magazines, no alphabets — even no pictures.

Of all the aboriginal peoples that remain in North

America, none is richer in folk-lore than the Pueblo Indians of New Mexico, who are, I believe, next to the largest of the native tribes left in the United States. They number nine thousand souls. They have nineteen "cities" (called pueblos, also) in this Territory, and seven in Arizona; and each has its little outlying colonies. They are not cities in size, it is true, for the largest (Zuñi) has only fifteen hundred people, and the smallest only about one hundred; but cities they are, nevertheless. And each city, with its fields, is a wee republic — twenty-six of the smallest, and perhaps the oldest, republics in the world; for they were already such when the first European eyes saw America. Each has its governor, its congress, its sheriffs, war-captains, and other officials who are elected annually; its laws, unwritten but unalterable, which are more respected and better enforced than the laws of any American community; its permanent and very comfortable houses, and its broad fields, confirmed first by Spain and later by patents of the United States.

The architecture of the Pueblo houses is quaint and characteristic. In the remote pueblos they are as many as six stories in height — built somewhat in the shape of an enormous terraced pyramid. The Pueblos along the Rio Grande, however, have felt the influence of Mexican customs, and their houses have but one and two stories. All their buildings, including the huge, quaint church which each pueblo has, are made of stone plastered with adobe mud, or of great, sun-dried bricks of adobe. They are the most comfortable dwellings in the Southwest — cool in summer and warm in winter.

The Pueblos are divided into six tribes, each speaking a distinct language of its own. Isleta, the quaint village where I lived five years, in an Indian house, with Indian neighbors, and under Indian laws, is the southernmost of the pueblos, the next largest of them all, and the chief city of the Tée-wahn tribe.[1] All the languages of the Pueblo tribes are exceedingly difficult to learn.

Besides the cities now inhabited, the ruins of about fifteen hundred other pueblos — and some of them the noblest ruins in the country — dot the brown valleys and rocky mesa-tops of New Mexico. All these ruins are of stone, and are extremely interesting. The implacable savages by whom they were hemmed in made necessary the abandonment of hundreds of pueblos; and this great number of ruins does not indicate a vast ancient population. The Pueblos *never* counted above 30,000 souls.

The Pueblo Indians have for nearly two centuries given no trouble to the European sharers of their domain; but their wars of defense against the savage tribes who surrounded them completely — with the Apaches, Navajos, Comanches, and Utes — lasted until a very few years ago. They are valiant fighters for their homes, but prefer any honorable peace. They are not indolent, but industrious — tilling their farms, tending their stock, and keeping all their affairs in order. The women own the houses and their contents, and do not work outside; and the men control the fields and crops. An unhappy home is almost an unknown thing among them; and the universal affection of parents for

1 Spelled Tigua by Spanish authors.

children and respect of children for parents are extraordinary. I have never seen a child unkindly treated, a parent saucily addressed, or a playmate abused, in all my long and intimate acquaintance with the Pueblos.

Isleta lies on the Atlantic and Pacific Railroad, upon the western bank of the Rio Grande, on a lava promontory which was once an island — whence the town takes its Spanish name. Its Tée-wahn title is Shee-eh-whíb-bak.[1] Its population, according to the census taken in 1891, is a little less than twelve hundred. It is nearly surrounded by fertile vineyards, orchards of peaches, apricots, apples, cherries, plums, pears, and quinces, and fields of corn, wheat, beans, and peppers, all owned by my dusky neighbors. The pueblo owns over one hundred and ten thousand acres of land, the greater part of which is reserved for pasturing horses and cattle.

The people of Isleta are, as a rule, rather short in stature, but strongly built. All have a magnificent depth and breadth of chest, and a beautifully confident poise of the head. Most of the men are very expert hunters, tireless runners, and fine horsemen. Besides ordinary hunting they have communal hunts—for rabbits in the spring, for antelope and deer in the fall—thoroughly organized, in which great quantities of game are killed.

Their amusements are many and varied. Aside from the numerous sacred dances of the year, their most important occasions, they have various races

---

1 The name means "Knife-laid-on-the-ground-to-play-*whib*." *Whib* is an aboriginal foot-race in which the runners have to carry a stick with their toes. The name was perhaps suggested by the knife-like shape of the lava ridge on which the pueblo is built.

which call for great skill and endurance, quaint social enjoyments, and games of many kinds, some of which are quite as difficult as chess. They are very fair weavers and pottery-makers. The women are good housewives, and most of them excellent seamstresses.

Yet, with all this progress in civilization, despite their mental and physical acuteness and their excellent moral qualities, the Tée-wahn are in some things but overgrown children. Their secret inner religion[1] is one of the most complicated systems on earth. Besides the highest deities, all the forces of nature, all animals, as well as many things that are inanimate, are invested by them with supernatural powers. They do not worship idols, but images and tokens of unseen powers are revered. They do nothing without some reason, generally a religious one, and whatever they observe they can explain in their own superstitious way. Every custom they have and every belief they own has a reason which to them is all-sufficient; and for each they have a story. There is no duty to which a Pueblo child is trained in which he has to be content with the bare command, "Do thus"; for each he learns a fairy tale designed to explain how people first came to know that it was right to do thus, and detailing the sad results which befell those who did otherwise.

It is from this wonderful folk-lore of the Tée-wahn that I have learned—after long study of the people, their language, customs, and myths—and

[1] For they are all devout, if not entirely understanding, members of a Christian church; but keep alsu much of their prehistoric faiths.

taken, unchanged and unembellished, this series of
Indian fairy tales.   I have been extremely careful
to preserve, in my translations, the exact Indian
spirit.   An absolutely literal translation would be
almost unintelligible to English readers, but I have
taken no liberties with the real meaning.

The use of books is not only to tell, but to preserve ; not only for to-day, but for ever.   What an
Indian wishes to perpetuate must be saved by
tongue and ear, by "telling-down," as were the
world's first histories and poems.   This oral trans-
mission from father to son is of sacred importance
with the natives.   Upon it depends the preservation
of the amusements, the history, the beliefs, the customs, and the laws of their nation.   A people less
observant, less accurate of speech and of memory,
would make a sad failure of this sort of record; but
with them it is a wonderful success.   The story
goes down from generation to generation, almost
without the change of a word.   The fact that it is
told in fixed metrical form—a sort of blank verse
—helps the memory.

Here in Isleta, the quaint pueblo of the Tée-
wahn, I became deeply interested not only in the
folk-stories themselves, but also in the manner of
handing them down.   Winter is the season for
story-telling.   Then the thirsty fields no longer cry
for water, the irrigating-ditches have ceased to
gnaw at their banks, and the men are often at
leisure.   Then, of an evening, if I go over to visit
some *vecino* (neighbor), I am likely to find, in the
great adobe living-room, a group of very old men
and very young boys gathered about the queer little

"AS I COME IN, KINDLY OLD TATA LORENSO IS JUST BEGINNING A STORY."

corner fireplace with its blazing upright sticks. They, too, have come a-visiting. The young men are gathered in another corner by themselves, eating roasted corn, and talking in whispers so as not to disturb their elders, for respect to age is the corner-stone of all Indian training. They are not required to listen to the stories, being supposed to know them already.

If in the far, sweet days when I stood at my grandmother's knee, and shivered over " Bluebeard," or thrilled at " Jack the Giant-killer," some one could have shown us a picture of me as I was to be listening to other fairy tales twenty-five years later, I am sure that her eyes would have opened wide as mine. Certainly neither of us ever dreamed that, thousands of miles from the old New England fireplace, when the dear figures that sat with me before its blazing forestick had long been dust, I would be sitting where I am to-night and listening to the strange, dark people who are around me. The room is long and low, and overhead are dark, round rafters — the trunks of straight pine-trees that used to purr on the sides of the most famous mountain in New Mexico. The walls are white as snow, and you would never imagine that they are built only of cut sods, plastered over and whitewashed. The floor is of adobe clay, packed almost as hard as a rock, and upon it are bright-hued blankets, woven in strange figures. Along the walls are benches, with wool mattresses rolled up and laid upon them. By and by these will be spread upon the floor for beds, but just now they

serve as cushioned seats.   Over in a corner are
strange earthen jars of water, with little gourd dippers floating, and here and there upon the wall
hang bows and arrows in sheaths of the tawny hide
of the mountain lion; queer woven belts of red and
green, and heavy necklaces of silver and coral, with
charms of turquoise — the stone that stole its color
from the sky.

There is a fireplace, too, and we are gathered all
about it, a dozen or more — for I have become an
old friend here.   But it is not like the fireplace
where the little sister and I used to roast our apples and pop our corn.   A wee hearth of clay rises
a few inches from the floor; a yard above it hangs
the chimney, like a big white hood; and a little
wall, four feet high, runs from it out into the room,
that the wind from the outer door may not blow
the ashes.   There is no big front log, but three or
four gnarled cedar sticks, standing on one end,
crackle loudly.

Some of us are seated on benches, and upon the
floor.   His back against the wall, squats my host,
who is just going to begin another fairy story.
Such a wee, withered, wrinkled old man!   It seems
as though the hot winds of the Southwest had dried
him as they dry the forgotten last year's apples
that shrivel here and there upon lonely boughs.
He must be a century old.   His children, grandchildren, great-grandchildren, and great-great-
grandchildren are all represented here to-night.
Yet his black eyes are like a hawk's, under their
heavy brows, and his voice is musical and deep.
I have never heard a more eloquent story-teller,

and I have heard some famous ones. I can tell you the words, but not the impressive tones, the animation of eye and accent, the eloquent gestures of this venerable Indian as he tells — what? An Indian telling fairy stories?

Yes, indeed. He is the very man to tell them. If this dusky old playground for wrinkles, who never saw the inside of a book, could write out all the fairy stories he knows, Webster's Unabridged Dictionary would hardly hold them. His father and his father's father, and so on back for countless centuries, have handed down these stories by telling, from generation to generation, just as Tata[1] Lorenso is telling his great-great-grandsons to-night. When these boys grow up, they will tell these stories to their sons and grandsons; and so the legends will pass on and on, so long as there shall be a Tée-wahn Indian left in all New Mexico.

But Lorenso is ready with his story. He pauses only to make a cigarette from the material in my pouch (they call me *Por todos*, because I have tobacco "for all"), explains for my benefit that this is a story of the beginning of Isleta, pats the head of the chubby boy at his knee, and begins again.

1 " Father."

I

THE ANTELOPE BOY

ONCE upon a time there were two towns of the Tée-wahn, called Nah-bah-tóo-too-ee (white village) and Nah-choo-rée-too-ee (yellow village). A man of Nah-bah-tóo-too-ee and his wife were attacked by Apaches while out on the plains one day, and took refuge in a cave, where they were besieged. And there a boy was born to them. The father was killed in an attempt to return to his village for help; and starvation finally forced the mother to crawl forth by night seeking roots to eat. Chased by the Apaches, she escaped to her own village, and it was several days before she could return to the cave—only to find it empty.

The baby had begun to cry soon after her departure. Just then a Coyote[1] was passing, and heard. Taking pity on the child, he picked it up and carried it across the plain until he came to a herd of antelopes. Among them was a Mother-Antelope that had lost her fawn; and going to her the Coyote said:

"Here is an *ah-bóo* (poor thing) that is left by its people. Will you take care of it?"

[1] The small prairie-wolf.

The Mother-Antelope, remembering her own baby, with tears said " Yes," and at once adopted the tiny stranger, while the Coyote thanked her and went home.

So the boy became as one of the antelopes, and grew up among them until he was about twelve years old. Then it happened that a hunter came out from Nah-bah-tóo-too-ee for antelopes, and found this herd. Stalking them carefully, he shot one with an arrow. The rest started off, running like the wind; but ahead of them all, as long as they were in sight, he saw a boy! The hunter was much surprised, and, shouldering his game, walked back to the village, deep in thought. Here he told the Cacique[1] what he had seen. Next day the crier was sent out to call upon all the people to prepare for a great hunt, in four days, to capture the Indian boy who lived with the antelopes.

While preparations were going on in the village, the antelopes in some way heard of the intended hunt and its purpose. The Mother-Antelope was very sad when she heard it, and at first would say nothing. But at last she called her adopted son to her and said: "Son, you have heard that the people of Nah-bah-tóo-too-ee are coming to hunt. But they will not kill us; all they wish is to take you. They will surround us, intending to let all the antelopes escape from the circle. You must follow me where I break through the line, and your real mother will be coming on the northeast side in a white *manta* (robe). I will pass close to her, and you must stagger and fall where she can catch you."

[1] The highest religious official.

On the fourth day all the people went out upon
the plains.   They found and surrounded the herd
of antelopes, which ran about in a circle when the
hunters closed upon them.   The circle grew smaller,
and the antelopes began to break through; but the
hunters paid no attention to them, keeping their
eyes upon the boy.   At last he and his antelope
mother were the only ones left, and when she
broke through the line on the northeast he followed her and fell at the feet of his own human
mother, who sprang forward and clasped him in
her arms.

Amid great rejoicing he was taken to Nah-bah-
tóo-too-ee, and there he told the *principales*[1] how
he had been left in the cave, how the Coyote had
pitied him, and how the Mother-Antelope had
reared him as her own son.

It was not long before all the country round
about heard of the Antelope Boy and of his marvel-
ous fleetness of foot.   You must know that the antelopes never comb their hair, and while among them
the boy's head had grown very bushy.   So the
people called him *Pée-hleh-o-wah-wée-deh* (big-
headed little boy).

Among the other villages that heard of his
prowess was Nah-choo-rée-too-ee, all of whose
people "had the bad road."[2]   They had a wonderful runner named *Pée-k'hoo* (Deer-foot), and very
soon they sent a challenge to Nah-bah-tóo-too-ee
for a championship race.   Four days were to be
given for preparation, to make bets, and the like.

---

[1] The old men who are the congress of the pueblo.
[2] That is, were witches.

THE COYOTE CARRIES THE BABY TO THE ANTELOPE MOTHER.

The race was to be around the world.[1] Each village was to stake all its property and the lives of all its people on the result of the race. So powerful were the witches of Nah-choo-rée-too-ee that they felt safe in proposing so serious a stake; and the people of Nah-bah-tóo-too-ee were ashamed to decline the challenge.

The day came, and the starting-point was surrounded by all the people of the two villages, dressed in their best. On each side were huge piles of ornaments and dresses, stores of grain, and all the other property of the people. The runner for the yellow village was a tall, sinewy athlete, strong in his early manhood; and when the Antelope Boy appeared for the other side, the witches set up a howl of derision, and began to strike their rivals and jeer at them, saying, "Pooh! We might as well begin to kill you now! What can that *óo-deh* (little thing) do?"

At the word "*Hái-ko!*" ("Go!") the two runners started toward the east like the wind. The Antelope Boy soon forged ahead; but Deer-foot, by his witchcraft, changed himself into a hawk and flew lightly over the lad, saying, "*We* do this way to each other!"[2] The Antelope Boy kept running, but his heart was very heavy, for he knew that no feet could equal the swift flight of the hawk.

---

[1] The Pueblos believed it was an immense plain whereon the racers were to race over a square course — to the extreme east, then to the extreme north, and so on, back to the starting-point.

[2] A common Indian taunt, either good-natured or bitter, to the loser of a game or to a conquered enemy.

2

But just as he came half-way to the east, a Mole
came up from its burrow and said :

"My son, where are you going so fast with a
sad face?"

The lad explained that the race was for the

RAIN FALLS ON PÉE-K'HOO.

property and lives of all his people ; and that the
witch-runner had turned to a hawk and left him far
behind.

"Then, my son," said the Mole, "I will be he that shall help you. Only sit down here a little while, and I will give you something to carry."

The boy sat down, and the Mole dived into the hole, but soon came back with four cigarettes.[1]

Holding them out, the Mole said, "Now, my son, when you have reached the east and turned north, smoke one; when you have reached the north and turn west, smoke another; when you turn south, another, and when you turn east again, another. *Hái-ko!*"

The boy ran on, and soon reached the east. Turning his face to the north he smoked the first cigarette. No sooner was it finished than he became a young antelope; and at the same instant a furious rain began. Refreshed by the cool drops, he started like an arrow from the bow. Half-way to the north he came to a large tree; and there sat the hawk, drenched and chilled, unable to fly, and crying piteously.

"Now, friend, *we* too do this to each other," called the boy-antelope as he dashed past. But just as he reached the north, the hawk — which had become dry after the short rain — caught up and passed him, saying, "We too do this to each other!" The boy-antelope turned westward, and smoked the second cigarette; and at once another terrific rain began.[2] Half-way to the west he again passed the hawk shivering and crying in a tree,

1 These are made by putting a certain weed called *pee-én-hleh* into hollow reeds.

2 I should state, by the way, that the cigarette plays an important part in the Pueblo folk-stories, — they never had the pipe of the Northern Indians, — and all rain-clouds are supposed to come from its smoke.

and unable to fly; but as he was about to turn to
the south, the hawk passed him with the customary taunt.   The smoking of the third cigarette
brought another storm, and again the antelope
passed the wet hawk half-way, and again the hawk
dried its feathers in time to catch up and pass him
as he was turning to the east for the home-stretch.
Here again the boy-antelope stopped and smoked
a cigarette — the fourth and last.   Again a short,

"THE TWO RUNNERS CAME SWEEPING DOWN THE HOME-STRETCH,
STRAINING EVERY NERVE."

hard rain came, and again he passed the water-
bound hawk half-way.

Knowing the witchcraft of their neighbors, the
people of Nah-bah-tóo-too-ee had made the condition that, in whatever shape the racers might run the
rest of the course, they must resume human form
upon arrival at a certain hill upon the fourth turn,
which was in sight of the goal.   The last wetting
of the hawk's feathers delayed it so that the antelope reached the hill just ahead; and there, resum-
ing their natural shapes, the two runners came

sweeping down the home-stretch, straining every
nerve.   But the Antelope Boy gained at each
stride.   When they saw him, the witch-people felt
confident that he was their champion, and again
began to push, and taunt, and jeer at the others.
But when the little Antelope Boy sprang lightly
across the line, far ahead of Deer-foot, their joy
turned to mourning.

The people of Nah-bah-tóo-too-ee burned all
the witches upon the spot, in a great pile of corn;
but somehow one escaped, and from him come all
the witches that trouble us to this day.

The property of the witches was taken to Nah-
bah-tóo-too-ee; and as it was more than that village could hold, the surplus was sent to Shee-eh-
whíb-bak (Isleta), where we enjoy it to this day;
and later the people themselves moved here.   And
even now, when we dig in that little hill on the
other side of the *charco* (pool), we find charred
corn-cobs, where our forefathers burned the witch-
people of the yellow village.

During Lorenso's story the black eyes of the boys
have never left his face; and at every pause they
have made the customary response, " Is that so ? "
to show their attention; while the old men have
nodded approbation, and smoked in deep silence.

Now Lorenso turns to Desiderio,[1] who is far
more wrinkled even than he, and says, " You have
a tail, brother."   And Desiderio, clearing his
throat and making a new cigarette with great im-
pressiveness, begins: " My sons, do you know why
the Coyote and the Crows are always at war?
No ?   Then I will tell you."

1 Pronounced Day-see-dáy-ree-oh.

II

THE COYOTE AND THE CROWS

ONCE on a time many Káh-ahn lived in the edge of some woods. A little out into the plain stood a very large tree, with much sand under it. One day a Coyote was passing, and heard the Crows singing and dancing under this tree, and came up to watch them. They were dancing in a circle, and each Crow had upon his back a large bag.

"Crow-friends, what are you doing?" asked the Coyote, who was much interested.

"Oh, we are dancing with our mothers," said the Crows.

"How pretty! And will you let me dance, too?" asked the Coyote of the *too-whit-lah-wid-deh* crow (captain of the dance).

"Oh, yes," replied the Crow. "Go and put your mother in a bag and come to the dance."

The Coyote went running home. There his old mother was sitting in the corner of the fireplace. The stupid Coyote picked up a stick and struck her on the head, and put her in a bag, and hurried back to the dance with her.

The Crows were dancing merrily, and singing: *"Ai nana, que-ée-rah, que-ée-rah."* ("Alas, Mama!

you are shaking, you are shaking!") The Coyote
joined the dance, with the bag on his back, and
sang as the Crows did:

"*Ai nana, que-ée-rah, que-ée-rah.*" [1]

But at last the Crows burst out laughing, and
said, "What do you bring in your bag?"

"My mother, as you told me," replied the Coyote, showing them.

Then the Crows emptied their bags, which were
filled with nothing but sand, and flew up into the
tree, laughing.

The Coyote then saw that they had played him
a trick, and started home, crying "*Ai nana!*"
When he got home he took his mother from the
bag and tried to set her up in the chimney-corner,
always crying, "*Ai nana,* why don't you sit up as
before?" But she could not, for she was dead.
When he found that she could not sit up any more,
he vowed to follow the Crows and eat them all the
rest of his life; and from that day to this he has
been hunting them, and they are always at war.

As Desiderio concludes, the old men hitch their
blankets around their shoulders. "No more stories
to-night?" I ask; and Lorenso says:

"*In-dáh* (no). Now it is to go to bed. *Tóo-kwai*
(come)," to the boys. "Good night, friends. Another time, perhaps."

And we file out through the low door into the
starry night.

[1] *Ai nana* is an exclamation always used by mourners.

III

THE WAR-DANCE OF THE MICE

TO-NIGHT it is withered Diego[1] who begins
with his story, in the musical but strange
Tée-wahn tongue, of " Shée-choon t'o-ah-fuar."
Serious as that looks, it means only "the war-
dance of the Mice."

Once upon a time there was war between the
people of Isleta and the Mice. There was a great
battle, in which the Tée-wahn killed many Mice
and took their scalps. Then the Tée-wahn returned to their village, and the warriors went into
the *estufa* (sacred council-chamber) to prepare
themselves by fasting for the great scalp-dance
in twelve days. While the warriors were sitting
inside, the Mice came secretly by night to attack
the town, and their spies crept up to the *estufa*.
When all the Tée-wahn warriors had fallen asleep,
the Mice came stealing down the big ladder into
the room, and creeping from sleeper to sleeper, they
gnawed every bowstring and cut the feathers from
the arrows and the strap of every sling. When
this was done, the Mice raised a terrible war-whoop
and rushed upon the warriors, brandishing their

1 Pronounced Dee-áy-go.

spears. The Tée-wahn woke and caught up their bows and arrows, but only to find them useless. So the warriors could do nothing but run from their tiny foes, and up the ladder to the roof they rushed pell-mell and thence fled to their homes, leaving the Mice victorious.

The rest of the town made such fun of the warriors that they refused to return to the fight; and the elated Mice held a public dance in front of the *estufa*. A brave sight it was, the army of these little people, singing and dancing and waving their spears. They were dressed in red blankets, with leather leggings glistening with silver buttons from top to bottom, and gay moccasins. Each had two eagle feathers tied to the top of his spear — the token of victory. And as they danced and marched and counter-marched, they sang exultingly:

> *Shée-oh-pah ch'-ót-im!*
> *Neh-máh-hlee-oh ch'-ot-im!*
> *Hló-tu feé-ny p'-óh-teh!*

over and over again—which means

> Quick we cut the bowstring!
> Quick we cut the sling-strap!
> We shaved the arrow-feathers off!

For four days they danced and sang, and on the night of the fourth day danced all night around a big bonfire. The next morning they marched away. That was the time when the Mice conquered men; and that is the reason why we have never been able to drive the Mice out of our homes to this day.

"Is *that* the reason?" ask all the boys, who have been listening with big black eyes intent.

"That is the very reason," says withered Diego. "Now, *compadre* Antonio, there is a tail to you."

Antonio, thus called upon, cannot refuse. Indian etiquette is very strict upon this point — as well as upon all others. So he fishes in his memory for a story, while the boys turn expectant faces toward him. He is not nearly so wrinkled as Diego, but he is very, very old, and his voice is a little tremulous at first. Wrapping his blanket about him, he begins :

Then I will tell you why the Coyote and the Blackbirds are enemies—for once they were very good friends in the old days.

IV

THE COYOTE AND THE BLACKBIRDS

ONCE upon a time a Coyote lived near an open wood. As he went to walk one day near the edge of the wood, he heard the Blackbirds (the Indian name means " seeds of the prairie ") calling excitedly :

" Bring my bag! Bring my bag! It is going to hail ! "

The Coyote, being very curious, came near and saw that they all had buckskin bags to which they were tying lassos, the other ends of which were thrown over the boughs of the trees. Very much surprised, the Coyote came to them and asked :

" Blackbird-friends, what are you doing ? "

" Oh, friend Coyote," they replied, " we are making ourselves ready, for soon there will be a very hard hail-storm, and we do not wish to be pelted to death. We are going to get into these bags and pull ourselves up under the branches, where the hail cannot strike us."

" That is very good," said the Coyote, " and I would like to do so, too, if you will let me join you."

" Oh, yes! Just run home and get a bag and a lasso, and come back here and we will help you," said the Pah-táhn, never smiling.

So the Coyote started running for home, and got a large bag and a lasso, and came back to the Blackbirds, who were waiting. They fixed the rope and bag for him, putting the noose around the neck of the bag so that it would be closed tight when the rope was pulled. Then they threw the end of the lasso over a strong branch and said :

"Now, friend Coyote, you get into your bag first, for you are so big and heavy that you cannot pull yourself up, and we will have to help you."

The Coyote crawled into the bag, and all the Blackbirds taking hold of the rope, pulled with all their might till the bag was swung clear up under the branch. Then they tied the end of the lasso around the tree so the bag could not come down, and ran around picking up all the pebbles they could find.

"Mercy! How the hail comes!" they cried excitedly, and began to throw stones at the swinging bag as hard as ever they could.

"Mercy!" howled the Coyote, as the pebbles pattered against him. "But this is a terrible storm, Blackbird-friends! It pelts me dreadfully! And how are you getting along?"

"It is truly very bad, friend Coyote," they answered, "but you are bigger and stronger than we, and ought to endure it." And they kept pelting him, all the time crying and chattering as if they, too, were suffering greatly from the hail.

"Ouch!" yelled the Coyote. "That one hit me very near the eye, friends! I fear this evil storm will kill us all!"

"But be brave, friend," called back the Black-birds. "We keep our hearts, and so should you, for you are much stronger than we." And they pelted him all the harder.

So they kept it up until they were too tired to throw any more; and as for the Coyote, he was so bruised and sore that he could hardly move. Then they untied the rope and let the bag slowly to the ground, and loosened the noose at the neck and flew up into the trees with sober faces.

"Ow!" groaned the Coyote, "I am nearly dead!" And he crawled weeping and groaning from the bag, and began to lick his bruises. But when he looked around and saw the sun shining and the ground dry, and not a hailstone anywhere, he knew that the Blackbirds had given him a trick, and he limped home in a terrible rage, vowing that as soon as ever he got well he would follow and eat the Blackbirds as long as he lived. And ever since, even to this day, he has been following them to eat them, and that is why the Coyote and the Blackbirds are always at war.

"Is that so?" cried all the boys in chorus, their eyes shining like coals.

"Oh, yes, that is the cause of the war," said old Antonio, gravely. "And now, brother, there is a tail to you," turning to the tall, gray-haired Felipe[1]; and clearing his throat, Felipe begins about the Coyote and the Bear.

1 Pronounced Fay-lée-peh.

V

THE COYOTE AND THE BEAR [1]

ONCE upon a time Ko-íd-deh (the Bear) and Too-wháy-deh (the Coyote) chanced to meet at a certain spot, and sat down to talk. After a while the Bear said:

"Friend Coyote, do you see what good land this is here? What do you say if we farm it together, sharing our labor and the crop?"

The Coyote thought well of it, and said so; and after talking, they agreed to plant potatoes in partnership.

"Now," said the Bear, "I think of a good way to divide the crop. I will take all that grows below the ground, and you take all that grows above it. Then each can take away his share when he is ready, and there will be no trouble to measure."

The Coyote agreed, and when the time came they plowed the place with a sharp stick and planted their potatoes. All summer they worked together in the field, hoeing down the weeds with stone hoes and letting in water now and then from the irrigating-ditch. When harvest-time came, the Coyote went and cut off all the potato-tops at the

[1] The Coyote, you must know, is very stupid about some things; and in almost all Pueblo fairy stories is the victim of one joke or another. The bear, on the other hand, is one of the wisest of animals.

ground and carried them home, and afterward the Bear scratched out the potatoes from the ground with his big claws and took them to his house. When the Coyote saw this his eyes were opened, and he said:

"But this is not fair. You have those round things, which are good to eat, but what I took home we cannot eat at all, neither my wife nor I."

"But, friend Coyote," answered the Bear, gravely, "did we not make an agreement? Then we must stick to it like men."

The Coyote could not answer, and went home; but he was not satisfied.

The next spring, as they met one day, the Bear said:

"Come, friend Coyote, I think we ought to plant this good land again, and this time let us plant it in corn. But last year you were dissatisfied with your share, so this year we will change. You take what is below the ground for your share, and I will take only what grows above."

This seemed very fair to the Coyote, and he agreed. They plowed and planted and tended the corn; and when it came harvest-time the Bear gathered all the stalks and ears and carried them home. When the Coyote came to dig his share, he found nothing but roots like threads, which were good for nothing. He was very much dissatisfied; but the Bear reminded him of their agreement, and he could say nothing.

That winter the Coyote was walking one day by the river (the Rio Grande), when he saw the Bear sitting on the ice and eating a fish. The Coyote was very fond of fish, and coming up, he said:

"Friend Bear, where did you get such a fat fish?"

"Oh, I broke a hole in the ice," said the Bear, "and fished for them. There are many here." And he went on eating, without offering any to the Coyote.

"Won't you show me how, friend?" asked the Coyote, fainting with hunger at the smell of the fish.

"Oh, yes," said the Bear. "It is very easy." And he broke a hole in the ice with his paw. "Now, friend Coyote, sit down and let your tail hang in the water, and very soon you will feel a nibble. But you must not pull it till I tell you."

So the Coyote sat down with his tail in the cold water. Soon the ice began to form around it, and he called:

"Friend Bear, I feel a bite! Let me pull him out."

"No, no! Not yet!" cried the Bear, "wait till he gets a good hold, and then you will not lose him."

So the Coyote waited. In a few minutes the hole was frozen solid, and his tail was fast.

"Now, friend Coyote," called the Bear, "I think you have him. Pull!"

The Coyote pulled with all his might, but could not lift his tail from the ice, and there he was — a prisoner. While he pulled and howled, the Bear shouted with laughter, and rolled on the ice and ha-ha'd till his sides were sore. Then he took his fish and went home, stopping every little to laugh at the thought of the Coyote.

There on the ice the Coyote had to stay until a thaw liberated him, and when he got home he was very wet and cold and half starved. And from that day to this he has never forgiven the Bear, and will not even speak to him when they meet, and the Bear says, politely, " Good morning, friend Too-wháy-deh."

" Is that so?" cry the boys.

"That is so," says Felipe. " But now it is time to go home. *Tóo-kwai !*"

The story-telling is over for to-night. Grandmother Reyes is unrolling the mattresses upon the floor; and with pleasant " good-nights" we scatter for our homes here and there in the quaint adobe village.

VI

"NOW there is a tail to you, *compadre* [friend]," said old Desiderio, nodding at Patricio[1] after we had sat awhile in silence around the crackling fire.

Patricio had a broad strip of rawhide across his knee, and was scraping the hair from it with a dull knife. It was high time to be thinking of new soles, for already there was a wee hole in the bottom of each of his moccasins; and as for Benito, his shy little grandson, *his* toes were all abroad.

But shrilly as the cold night-wind outside hinted the wisdom of speedy cobbling, Patricio had no wish

[1] Pronounced Pah-trée-see-oh.

34

to acquire that burro's tail, so, laying the rawhide and knife upon the floor beside him, he deliberately rolled a modest pinch of the aromatic *koo-ah-rée* in a corn-husk, lighted it at the coals, and drew Benito's tousled head to his side.

"You have heard," he said, with a slow puff, "about Nah-chu-rú-chu, the mighty medicine-man who lived here in Isleta in the times of the ancients?"

"*Ah-h!*" (Yes) cried all the boys. "You have promised to tell us how he married the moon!"

"Another time I will do so. But now I shall tell you something that was before that — for Nah-chu-rú-chu had many strange adventures before he married Páh-hlee-oh, the Moon-Mother. Do you know why the rattlesnake— which is the king of all snakes and alone has the power of death in his mouth — always shakes his *guaje*[1] before he bites?"

"*Een-dah!*" chorused Ramón and Benito, and Fat Juan, and Tomás,[2] very eagerly; for they were particularly fond of hearing about the exploits of the greatest of Tée-wahn medicine-men.

"Listen, then, and you shall hear."

In those days Nah-chu-rú-chu had a friend who lived in a pueblo nearer the foot of the Eagle-Feather Mountain than this, in the Place of the Red Earth, where still are its ruins; and the two young men went often to the mountain together to bring wood and to hunt. Now, Nah-chu-rú-

1 The Pueblo sacred rattle.
2 Pronounced Rah-móhn, Bay-née-toh, Whahn, Toh-máhs.

chu had a white heart, and never thought ill; but
the friend had the evil road and became jealous,
for Nah-chu-rú-chu was a better hunter. But he
said nothing, and made as if he still loved Nah-
chu-rú-chu truly.

One day the friend came over from his village
and said:

"Friend Nah-chu-rú-chu, let us go to-morrow
for wood and to have a hunt.

"It is well," replied Nah-chu-rú-chu. Next
morning he started very early and came to the village of his friend; and together they went to the
mountain. When they had gathered much wood,
and lashed it in bundles for carrying, they started
off in opposite directions to hunt. In a short time
each returned with a fine fat deer.

"But why should we hasten to go home, friend
Nah-chu-rú-chu?" said the friend. "It is still early,
and we have much time. Come, let us stop here
and amuse ourselves with a game."

"It is well, friend," answered Nah-chu-rú-chu;
"but what game shall we play? For we have
neither *pa-toles*, nor hoops, nor any other game
here."

"See! we will roll the *mah-khúr*,[1] for while I
was waiting for you I made one that we might
play" — and the false friend drew from beneath his
blanket a pretty painted hoop; but really he had

1 The game of *mah-khúr*, which the Pueblos learned from the Apaches many
centuries ago, is a very simple one, but is a favorite with all witches as a snare
for those whom they would injure. A small hoop of willow is painted gaily,
and has ornamental buckskin thongs stretched across it from side to side,
spoke-fashion. The challenger to a game rolls the hoop rapidly past the challenged, who must throw a lance through between the spokes before it ceases
to roll.

"AS HE CAUGHT THE HOOP HE WAS INSTANTLY CHANGED INTO
A POOR COYOTE!"

made it at home, and had brought it hidden, on purpose to do harm to Nah-chu-rú-chu.

"Now go down there and catch it when I roll it," said he; and Nah-chu-rú-chu did so. But as he caught the hoop when it came rolling, he was no longer Nah-chu-rú-chu the brave hunter, but a poor Coyote with great tears rolling down his nose!

"Hu!" said the false friend, tauntingly, "we do this to each other! So now you have all the plains to wander over, to the north, and west, and south; but you can never go to the east. And if you are not lucky, the dogs will tear you; but if you are lucky, they may have pity on you. So now good-by, for this is the last I shall ever see of you."

Then the false friend went away, laughing, to his village; and the poor Coyote wandered aimlessly, weeping to think that he had been betrayed by the one he had loved and trusted as a brother. For four days he prowled about the outskirts of Isleta, looking wistfully at his home. The fierce dogs ran out to tear him; but when they came near they only sniffed at him, and went away without hurting him. He could find nothing to eat save dry bones, and old thongs or soles of moccasins.

On the fourth day he turned westward, and wandered until he came to Mesita.[1] There was no town of the Lagunas there then, and only a shepherd's hut and corral, in which were an old Quères Indian and his grandson, tending their goats.

Next morning when the grandson went out very early to let the goats from the corral, he saw a Coyote run out from among the goats. It went

---

[1] An outlying colony of Laguna, forty miles from Isleta.

off a little way, and then sat down and watched
him.   The boy counted the goats, and none were
missing, and he thought it strange.   But he said
nothing to his grandfather.

For three more mornings the very same thing
happened; and on the fourth morning the boy told
his grandfather.   The old man came out, and set
the dogs after the Coyote, which was sitting a little
way off; but when they came near they would not
touch him.

"I suspect there is something wrong here," said
the old shepherd; and he called: "Coyote, are you
coyote-true, or are you people?"

But the Coyote could not answer; and the old
man called again: "Coyote, are you people?"

At that the Coyote nodded his head, "Yes."

"If that is so, come here and be not afraid of
us; for we will be the ones to help you out of this
trouble."

So the Coyote came to them and licked their
hands, and they gave it food — for it was dying of
hunger.   When it was fed, the old man said:

"Now, son, you are going out with the goats
along the creek, and there you will see some willows.   With your mind look at two willows, and
mark them; and to-morrow morning you must go
and bring one of them."

The boy went away tending the goats, and the
Coyote stayed with the old man.   Next morning,
when they awoke very early, they saw all the earth
wrapped in a white *manta*.[1]

---

[1] This figure is always used by the Pueblos in speaking of snow in connection with sacred things.

"COYOTE, ARE YOU PEOPLE?"

" Now, son," said the old man, " you must wear
only your moccasins and breech-clout, and go like a
man to the two willows you marked yesterday. To
one of them you must pray; and then cut the other
and bring it to me."

The boy did so and came back with the willow
stick. The old man prayed, and made a *mah-khúr*
hoop ; and bidding the Coyote stand a little way
off and stick his head through the hoop before it
should stop rolling, rolled it toward him. The
Coyote waited till the hoop came very close, and
gave a great jump and put his head through it before it could stop. And lo! there stood Nah-chu-
rú-chu, young and handsome as ever ; but his
beautiful suit of fringed buckskin was all in rags.
For four days he stayed there and was cleansed
with the cleansing of the medicine-man ; and then
the old shepherd said to him :

" Now, friend Nah-chu-rú-chu, there is a road.[1]
But take with you this *faja*,[2] for though your
power is great, you have submitted to this evil.
When you get home, he who did this to you will
be first to know, and he will come pretending to be
your friend, as if he had done nothing ; and he will
ask you to go hunting again. So you must go ;
and when you come to the mountain, with this *faja*
you shall repay him."

Nah-chu-rú-chu thanked the kind old shepherd,
and started home. But when he came to the Bad
Hill and looked down into the valley of the Rio
Grande, his heart sank. All the grass and

---

[1] That is, you can go home.
[2] A fine woven belt, with figures in red and green.

fields and trees were dry and dead — for Nah-chu-rú-chu was the medicine-man who controlled the clouds, so no rain could fall when he was gone; and the eight days he had been a Coyote were in truth eight years. The river was dry, and the springs; and many of the people were dead from thirst, and the rest were dying. But as Nah-chu-rú-chu came down the hill, it began to rain again, and all the people were glad.

When he came into the pueblo, all the famishing people came out to welcome him. And soon came the false friend, making as if he had never bewitched him nor had known whither he disappeared.

In a few days the false friend came again to propose a hunt; and next morning they went to the mountain together. Nah-chu-rú-chu had the pretty *faja* wound around his waist; and when the wind blew his blanket aside, the other saw it.

"Ay! What a pretty *faja!*" cried the false friend. "Give it to me, friend Nah-chu-rú-chu."

"*Een-dah!*" (No) said Nah-chu-rú-chu. But the false friend begged so hard that at last he said:

"Then I will roll it to you; and if you can catch it before it unwinds, you may have it."

So he wound it up,[1] and holding by one end gave it a push so that it ran away from him, unrolling as it went. The false friend jumped for it, but it was unrolled before he caught it.

"*Een-dah!*" said Nah-chu-rú-chu, pulling it back. "If you do not care enough for it to be spryer than that, you cannot have it."

1 Like a roll of tape.

"AS HE SEIZED IT HE WAS CHANGED FROM A TALL YOUNG
MAN INTO A GREAT RATTLESNAKE."

The false friend begged for another trial; so Nah-chu-rú-chu rolled it again. This time the false friend caught it before it was unrolled; and lo! instead of a tall young man, there lay a great rattlesnake with tears rolling from his lidless eyes! "We, too, do this to each other!" said Nah-chu-rú-chu. He took from his medicine-pouch a pinch of the sacred meal and laid it on the snake's flat head for its food; and then a pinch of the corn-pollen to tame it.[1] And the snake ran out its red forked tongue, and licked them.

"Now," said Nah-chu-rú-chu, "this mountain and all rocky places shall be your home. But you can never again do to another harm, without warning, as you did to me. For see, there is a *guaje*[2] in your tail, and whenever you would do any one an injury, you must warn them beforehand with your rattle."

"And is that the reason why Ch'ah-rah-ráh-deh always rattles to give warning before he bites?" asked Fat Juan, who is now quite as often called Juan Biscocho (John Biscuit), since I photographed him one day crawling out of the big adobe bake-oven where he had been hiding.

"That is the very reason. Then Nah-chu-rú-chu left his false friend, from whom all the rattlesnakes are descended, and came back to his village. From that time all went well with Isleta, for Nah-chu-rú-chu was at home again to attend to the clouds. There was plenty of rain, and the river began to run again, and the springs flowed.

---

1 This same spell is still used here by the *Hee-hut-hái*, or snake-charmers.
2 Pronounced Gwáh-heh.

The people plowed and planted again, as they had
not been able to do for several years, and all their
work prospered.   As for the people who lived in
the Place of the Red Earth, they all moved down
here,[1] because the Apaches were very bad; and
here their descendants live to this day."

"Is that so?" sighed all the boys in chorus,
sorry that the story was so soon done.

"That is so," replied old Patricio.   "And now,
compadre Antonio, there is a tail to you."

"Well, then, I will tell a story which they
showed me in Taos[2] last year," said the old man.

"Ah-h!" said the boys.

"It is about the Coyote and the Woodpecker."

[1] It is a proved fact that there was such a migration.
[2] The most northern of the Pueblo cities.   Its people are also Tée-wahn.

VII

THE COYOTE AND THE WOODPECKER

WELL, once upon a time a Coyote and his family lived near the edge of a wood. There was a big hollow tree there, and in it lived an old Woodpecker and his wife and children. One day as the Coyote-father was strolling along the edge of the forest he met the Woodpecker-father.

"*Hin-no-kah-kée-ma*" (Good evening), said the Coyote; "how do you do to-day, friend Hloo-rée-deh?"

"Very well, thank you; and how are you, friend Too-wháy-deh?"

So they stopped and talked together awhile; and when they were about to go apart the Coyote said:

"Friend Woodpecker, why do you not come as friends to see us? Come to our house to supper this evening, and bring your family."

"Thank you, friend Coyote," said the Woodpecker; "we will come with joy."

So that evening, when the Coyote-mother had made supper ready, there came the Woodpecker-father and the Woodpecker-mother with their three children. When they had come in, all five of the Woodpeckers stretched themselves as they do after flying, and by that showed their pretty feathers — for the Hloo-rée-deh has yellow and red marks under its wings. While they were eating supper, too, they sometimes spread their

THE COYOTES AT SUPPER WITH THE WOODPECKERS.

wings, and displayed their bright under-side. They praised the supper highly, and said the Coyote-mother was a perfect housekeeper. When it was time to go, they thanked the Coy-otes very kindly and invited them to come to supper at their house the following evening. But when they were gone, the Coyote-father could hold himself no longer, and he said:

"Did you see what airs those Woodpeckers put on? Always showing off their bright feathers? But I want them to know that the Coyotes are equal to them. *I 'll* show them!"

Next day, the Coyote-father had all his family at work bringing wood, and built a great fire in front of his house. When it was time to go to the house of the Woodpeckers he called his wife and children to the fire, and lashed a burning stick under each of their arms, with the burning end pointing forward; and then he fixed himself in the same way.

"Now," said he, "we will show them! When we get there, you must lift up your arms now and then, to show them that we are as good as the Woodpeckers."

When they came to the house of the Woodpeckers and went in, all the Coyotes kept lifting their arms often, to show the bright coals underneath. But as they sat down to supper, one Coyote-girl gave a shriek and said:

"Oh, *tata!* My fire is burning me!"

"Be patient, my daughter," said the Coyote-father, severely, "and do not cry about little things."

"Ow!" cried the other Coyote-girl in a moment, "my fire has gone out!"

This was more than the Coyote-father could stand, and he reproved her angrily.

"But how is it, friend Coyote," said the Woodpecker, politely, "that your colors are so bright at first, but very soon become black?"

"Oh, that is the beauty of our colors," replied the Coyote, smothering his rage; "that they are not always the same—like other people's—but turn all shades."

But the Coyotes were very uncomfortable, and made an excuse to hurry home as soon as they could. When they got there, the Coyote-father whipped them all for exposing him to be laughed at. But the Woodpecker-father gathered his children around him, and said:

"Now, my children, you see what the Coyotes have done. Never in your life try to appear what you are not. Be just what you really are, and put on no false colors."

"Is that so?" cried the boys.

"That is so; and it is as true for people as for birds. Now, *tóo-kwai*—for it is bedtime."

VIII

MONG the principal heroes of the Tée-wahn folk-lore, I hear of none more frequently in the winter story-tellings to which my aboriginal neighbors admit me, than the mighty Nah-chu-rú-chu. To this day his name, which means "The Bluish Light of Dawn," is deeply revered by the quaint people who claim him as one of their forefathers. He had no parents, for he was created by the Trues themselves, and by them was given such extraordinary powers as were second only to their own. His wonderful

feats and startling adventures — as still related by
the believing Isleteños — would fill a volume. One
of these fanciful myths has interested me particularly, not only for its important bearing on certain
ethnological matters, but for its intrinsic qualities
as well. It is a thoroughly characteristic leaf from
the legendary lore of the Southwest.

Long before the first Spaniards came to New
Mexico (and *that* was three hundred and fifty
years ago) Isleta stood where it stands to-day
— on a lava ridge that defies the gnawing current
of the Rio Grande.[1] In those far days, Nah-chu-
rú-chu dwelt in Isleta, and was a leader of his
people. A weaver by trade,[2] his rude loom hung
from the dark rafters of his room; and in it he
wove the strong black *mantas* which are the dress
of Pueblo women to this day.

Besides being very wise in medicine, Nah-chu-
rú-chu was young, and tall, and strong, and handsome; and all the girls of the village thought it a
shame that he did not care to take a wife. For
him the shyest dimples played, for him the whitest
teeth flashed out, as the owners passed him in the
plaza; but he had no eyes for them. Then, in
the naïve custom of the Tée-wahn, bashful fingers
worked wondrous fringed shirts of buckskin, or
gay awl-sheaths, which found their way to his
house by unknown messengers — each as much as

1 Bandelier has published a contrary opinion, to which I do not think he
would now cling. The folk-lore and the very name of the town fully prove to
me that its site has not changed in historic times.
2 In the ancient days, weaving was practised only by the men, among the
Pueblos. This old usage is now reversed, and it is the women who weave,
except in the pueblos of Moqui.

to say, "She who made this is yours, if you will have her." But Nah-chu-rú-chu paid no more attention to the gifts than to the smiles, and just kept weaving and weaving—such *mantas* as were never seen in the land of the Tée-wahn before or since. The most persistent of his admirers were two sisters who were called *Ee-eh-chóo-ri-ch'áhm-nin* —the Yellow-Corn-Maidens. They were both young and pretty, but they "had the evil road" —which is the Indian way of saying that they were possessed of a magic power which they always used for ill. When all the other girls gave up, discouraged at Nah-chu-rú-chu's indifference, the Yellow-Corn-Maidens kept coming day after day, trying to attract him. At last the matter became such a nuisance to Nah-chu-rú-chu that he hired the deep-voiced town-crier to go through all the streets and announce that in four days Nah-chu-rú-chu would choose a wife.

For dippers, to take water from the big earthen *tinajas*, the Tée-wahn used then, as they use to-day, queer little ladle-shaped *omates* made of a gourd; but Nah-chu-rú-chu, being a great medi-cine-man and very rich, had a dipper of pure pearl, shaped like the gourds, but wonderfully precious.

"On the fourth day," proclaimed the crier, "Nah-chu-rú-chu will hang his pearl *omate* at his door, where every girl who will may throw a hand-ful of corn-meal at it. And she whose meal is so well ground that it sticks to the *omate*, she shall be the wife of Nah-chu-rú-chu!"

When this strange news came rolling down the still evening air, there was a great scampering of little moccasined feet. The girls ran out from hundreds of gray adobe houses to catch every word; and when the crier had passed on, they ran back into the store-rooms and began to ransack the corn-bins for the biggest, evenest, and most perfect ears. Shelling the choicest, each took her few handfuls of kernels to the sloping *metate*,[1] and

THE ISLETA GIRLS GRINDING CORN WITH THE "MANO"
ON THE "METATE."

with the *mano*, or hand-stone, scrubbed the grist up and down, and up and down, till the hard corn was a soft, blue meal. All the next day, and the next, and the next, they ground it over and over again, until it grew finer than ever flour was before; and every girl felt sure that her meal would stick to the *omate* of the handsome young weaver. The Yellow-Corn-Maidens worked hardest of all; day and night for four days they ground and ground, with all the magic spells they knew.

1 The slab of lava which still serves as a hand-mill in Pueblo houses.

Now, in those far-off days the Moon had not
gone up into the sky to live, but was a maiden of
Shee-eh-whíb-bak.   And a very beautiful girl she
was, though blind of one eye.   She had long admired
Nah-chu-rú-chu, but was always too maidenly to
try to attract his attention as other girls had done;
and at the time when the crier made his proclama-
tion, she happened to be
away at her father's ranch.
It was only upon the fourth
day that she returned to
town, and in a few moments
the girls were to go with
their meal to test it upon
the magic dipper.   The two
Yellow-Corn-Maidens were
just coming from their house
as she passed, and told her
of what was to be done.
They were very confident
of success, and told the
Moon-girl only to pain her;
and laughed derisively as
she went running to her
home.

THE MOON-MAIDEN.

By this time a long file
of girls was coming to Nah-
chu-rú-chu's house, outside
whose door hung the pearl
omate.   Each girl carried in
her left hand a little jar of
meal; and as they passed the door one by one, each
took from the jar a handful and threw it against

the magic dipper. But each time the meal dropped
to the ground, and left the pure pearl undimmed
and radiant as ever.

At last came the Yellow-Corn-Maidens, who had
waited to watch the failure of the others. As they
came where they could see Nah-chu-rú-chu sitting
at his loom, they called: "Ah! Here we have the
meal that will stick!" and each threw a handful at
the *omate*. But it did not stick at all; and still
from his seat Nah-chu-rú-chu could see, in that
mirror-like surface, all that went on outside.

The Yellow-Corn-Maidens were very angry, and
instead of passing on as the others had done, they
stood there and kept throwing and throwing at the
omate, which smiled back at them with undimin-
ished luster.

Just then, last of all, came the Moon, with a
single handful of meal which she had hastily ground.
The two sisters were in a fine rage by this time,
and mocked her, saying:

"Hoh! *P'áh-hlee-oh*,[1] you poor thing, we are very
sorry for you! Here we have been grinding our
meal four days and still it will not stick, and you
we did not tell till to-day. How, then, can you
ever hope to win Nah-chu-rú-chu? Pooh, you silly
little thing!"

But the Moon paid no attention whatever to
their taunts. Drawing back her little dimpled
hand, she threw the meal gently against the pearl
omate, and so fine was it ground that every tiniest
bit of it clung to the polished shell, and not a particle fell to the ground.

[1] Tée-wahn name of the moon; literally, "Water-Maiden."

THE YELLOW-CORN-MAIDENS THROWING MEAL AT THE PEARL "OMATE."

When Nah-chu-rú-chu saw that, he rose up quickly from his loom and came and took the Moon by the hand, saying, "You are she who shall be my wife.   You shall never want for anything, since I have very much." And he gave her many beautiful *mantas*, and cotton wraps, and fat boots of buckskin that wrap round and round, that she might dress as the wife of a rich chief.   But the Yellow-Corn-Maidens, who had seen it all, went away vowing vengeance on the Moon.

Nah-chu-rú-chu and his sweet Moon-wife were very happy together.   There was no other such housekeeper in all the pueblo as she, and no other hunter brought home so much buffalo-meat from the vast plains to the east, nor so many antelopes, and black-tailed deer, and jack-rabbits from the Manzanos as did Nah-chu-rú-chu.   But he constantly was saying to her:

"Moon-wife, beware of the Yellow-Corn-Maidens, for they have the evil road and will try to do you harm, but you must always refuse to do whatever they propose."   And always the young wife promised.

One day the Yellow-Corn-Maidens came to the house and said:

"Friend Nah-chu-rú-chu, we are going to the *llano*[1] to gather *amole*.[2]   Will you not let your wife go with us?"

"Oh, yes, she may go," said Nah-chu-rú-chu; but taking her aside, he said, "Now be sure that you refuse whatever they may propose."

1 Plain.
2 The soapy root of the palmilla, used for washing.

The Moon promised, and started away with the Yellow-Corn-Maidens.

In those days there was only a thick forest of cottonwoods where are now the smiling vineyards, and gardens, and orchards of Isleta, and to reach the *llano* the three women had to go through this forest. In the very center of it they came to a deep *pozo* — a square well, with steps at one side leading down to the water's edge.

"Ay!" said the Yellow-Corn-Maidens, "how hot and thirsty is our walk! Come, let us get a drink of water."

But the Moon, remembering her husband's words, said politely that she did not wish to drink. They urged in vain, but at last, looking down into the *pozo*, called:

"Oh, Moon-friend! Come and look in this still water, and see how pretty you are!"

The Moon, you must know, has always been just as fond of looking at herself in the water as she is to this very day, and forgetting Nah-chu-rú-chu's warning, she came to the brink, and looked down upon her fair reflection. But at that very moment, the two witch-sisters pushed her head foremost into the *pozo*, and drowned her; and then filled the well with earth, and went away as happy as wicked hearts can be.

Nah-chu-rú-chu began to look oftener from his loom to the door as the sun crept along the adobe floor, closer and closer to his seat; and when the shadows were very long, he sprang suddenly to his feet, and walked to the house of the Yellow-Corn-Maidens with long, strong strides.

"*Ee-eh-chóo-ri-ch'áhm-nin,*" he said, very sternly,
"where is my little wife?"

"Why, is n't she at home?" asked the wicked
sisters as if in great surprise. "She got enough
amole long before we did, and started home with it.
We supposed she had come long ago."

"Ah," groaned Nah-chu-rú-chu within himself;
"it is as I thought — they have done her ill." But
without a word to them he turned on his heel and
went away.

From that hour all went ill with Isleta, for Nah-
chu-rú-chu held the well-being of all his people,
even unto life and death. Paying no attention to
what was going on about him, he sat motionless
upon the very crosspiece of the *estufa* ladder — the
highest point in all the town — with his head
bowed upon his hands. There he sat for days,
never speaking, never moving. The children that
played along the streets looked up to the motionless figure, and ceased their boisterous play. The
old men shook their heads gravely, and muttered :
"We are in evil times, for Nah-chu-rú-chu is mourning, and will not be comforted. And there is no more
rain, so that our crops are drying in the fields.
What shall we do?"

At last all the councilors met together, and decided that there must be another effort made to
find the lost wife. It was true that the great Nah-
chu-rú-chu had searched for her in vain, and the
people had helped him; but perhaps some one else
might be more fortunate. So they took some of
the sacred smoking-weed wrapped in a corn-husk
and went to Shée-wid-deh, who has the sharpest

eyes in all the world. Giving him the sacred gift they said:

"Eagle-friend, we see Nah-chu-rú-chu in great trouble, for he has lost his Moon-wife. Come, search for her, we pray you, if she be alive or dead."

So the Eagle took the offering, and smoked the smoke-prayer; and then he went winging upward into the very sky. Higher and higher he rose, in great upward circles, while his keen eyes noted every stick, and stone, and animal on the face of all the world. But with all his eyes, he could see nothing of the lost wife; and at last he came back sadly, and said:

"People-friends, I went up to where I could see the whole world, but I could not find her."

Then the people went with an offering to the Coyote, whose nose is sharpest in all the world; and besought him to try to find the Moon. The Coyote smoked the smoke-prayer, and started off with his nose to the ground, trying to find her tracks. He trotted all over the earth; but at last he too came back without finding what he sought.

Then the troubled people got the Badger to search, for he is best of all the beasts at digging— and he it was whom the Trues employed to dig the caves in which the people first dwelt when they came to this world. The Badger trotted and pawed, and dug everywhere, but he could not find the Moon; and he came home very sad.

Then they asked the Osprey, who can see farthest under water, and he sailed high above all the lakes and rivers in the world, till he could count the

THE GRIEF OF NAH-CHU-RÚ-CHU.

pebbles and the fish in them, but he too failed to
discover the lost Moon.

By now the crops were dead and sere in the
fields, and thirsty animals walked crying along the
dry river. Scarcely could the people themselves dig
deep enough to find so much water as would keep
them alive. They were at a loss which way to turn;
but at last they thought: We will go to P'ah-kú-
ee-teh-áy-deh,[1] who can find the dead — for surely
she is dead, or the others would have found her.

So they went to him and besought him. The
Turkey-buzzard wept when he saw Nah-chu-rú-
chu still sitting there upon the ladder, and said:
"Truly it is sad for our great friend; but for me, I
am afraid to go, since they who are more mighty
than I have already failed; but I will try." And
spreading his broad wings he went climbing up the
spiral ladder of the sky. Higher he wheeled, and
higher, till at last not even the Eagle could see
him. Up and up, till the hot sun began to singe
his head, and not even the Eagle had ever been so
high. He cried with pain, but still he kept mount-
ing — until he was so close to the sun that all the
feathers were burned from his head and neck. But
he could see nothing; and at last, frantic with
the burning, he came wheeling downward. When
he got back to the *estufa* where all the people were
waiting, they saw that his head and neck had been
burnt bare of feathers — and from that day to this
the feathers would never grow out again.

"And did you see nothing?" they all asked,
when they had bathed his burns.

1 Turkey-buzzard; literally, "water-goose-grandfather."

"Nothing," he answered, "except that when I was half-way down I saw in the middle of yon cottonwood forest a little mound covered with all the beautiful flowers in the world."

"Oh!" cried Nah-chu-rú-chu, speaking for the first time. "Go, friend, and bring me one flower from the very middle of that mound."

Off flew the Buzzard, and in a few minutes returned with a little white flower. Nah-chu-rú-chu took it, and descending from the ladder in silence, walked to his house, while all the wondering people followed.

When Nah-chu-rú-chu came inside his home once more, he took a new *manta* and spread it in the middle of the room; and laying the wee white flower tenderly in its center, he put another new *manta* above it. Then, dressing himself in the splendid buckskin suit the lost wife had made him, and taking in his right hand the sacred *guaje* (rattle), he seated himself at the head of the *mantas* and sang:

> "*Shú-nah, shú-nah!*
> *Aí-ay-ay, aí-ay-ay, aí-ay-ay!*"

(Seeking her, seeking her!
There-away, there-away!)

When he had finished the song, all could see that the flower had begun to grow, so that it lifted the upper *manta* a little. Again he sang, shaking his gourd; and still the flower kept growing. Again and again he sang; and when he had finished for the fourth time, it was plain to all that a human form lay between the two *mantas*. And

when he sang his song the fifth time, the form sat
up and moved. Tenderly he lifted away the over-
cloth, and there sat his sweet Moon-wife, fairer than
ever, and alive as before! [1]

For four days the people danced and sang in the
public square. Nah-chu-rú-chu was happy again;
and now the rain began to fall. The choked earth
drank and was glad and green, and the dead crops
came to life.

When his wife told him how the witch-sisters
had done, he was very angry; and that very day
he made a beautiful hoop to play the *mah-khúr.*
He painted it, and put strings across it, decorated
with beaded buckskin.

"Now," said he, "the wicked Yellow-Corn-
Maidens will come to congratulate you, and will
pretend not to know where you were. You must
not speak of that, but invite them to go out and
play a game with you."

In a day or two the witch-sisters did come, with
deceitful words; and the Moon invited them to go
out and play a game. They went up to the edge
of the *llano*, and there she let them get a glimpse
of the pretty hoop.

"Oh, give us that, Moon-friend," they teased.
But she refused. At last, however, she said:

"Well, we will play the hoop-game. I will stand
here, and you there; and if, when I roll it to you,
you catch it before it falls upon its side, you may
have it."

---

1 Nah-chu-rú-chu's incantation followed the exact form still used by the
Indian conjurors of the Southwest in their wonderful trick of making corn
grow and mature from the kernel in one day.

So the witch-sisters stood a little way down the hill, and she rolled the bright hoop. As it came trundling to them, both grasped it at the same instant; and lo! instead of the Yellow-Corn-Maidens, there were two great snakes, with tears rolling down ugly faces. The Moon came and put upon their heads a little of the pollen of the corn-blossom (still used by Pueblo snake-charmers) to tame them, and a pinch of the sacred meal for their food.

"Now," said she, "you have the reward of treacherous friends. Here shall be your home among these rocks and cliffs forever, but you must never be found upon the prairie; and you must never bite a person. Remember you are women, and must be gentle."

And then the Moon went home to her husband, and they were very happy together. As for the sister snakes, they still dwell where she bade them, and never venture away; though sometimes the people bring them to their houses to catch the mice, for these snakes never hurt a person.

IX

THE MOTHER MOON

AND do you know why it is that the Moon has but one eye? It is a short story, but one of the most poetic and beautiful in all the pretty folk-lore of the Pueblos.

P'áh-hlee-oh, the Moon-Maiden, was the Tée-wahn Eve[1]—the first and loveliest woman in all the world. She had neither father nor mother, sister nor brother; and in her fair form were the seeds of all humanity—of all life and love and goodness. The Trues, who are the unseen spirits that are above all, made T'hoor-íd-deh, the Sun, who was to be father of all things; and because he was alone, they made for him a companion, the first to be of maids, the first to be a wife. From them began the world and all that is in it; and all their children were strong and good. Very happy were the Father-all and the Mother-all, as they watched their happy brood. He guarded them by day and

---

1 She is honored in almost every detail of the Pueblo ceremonials. The most important charm or implement of the medicine-men, the holiest fetish of all, is typical of her. It is called Mah-pah-róo, the Mother, and is the most beautiful article a Pueblo ever fashioned. A flawless ear of pure white corn (a type of fertility or motherhood) is tricked out with a downy mass of snow-white feathers, and hung with ornaments of silver, coral, and the precious turquoise.

she by night—only there *was* no night, for then
the Moon had two eyes, and saw as clearly as the
Sun, and with glance as bright.   It was all as one
long day of golden light.   The birds flew always,
the flowers never shut, the young people danced
and sang, and none knew how to rest.

But at last the Trues thought better.   For the
endless light grew heavy to the world's young eyes
that knew no tender lids of night.   And the Trues
said:

"It is not well, for so there is no sleep, and the
world is very tired.   We must not keep the Sun
and Moon seeing alike.   Let us put out one of his
eyes, that there may be darkness for half the time,
and then his children can rest."   And they called
T'hoor-íd-deh and P'áh-hlee-oh before them to say
what must be done.

But when she heard that, the Moon-Mother
wept for her strong and handsome husband, and
cried:

"No! No! Take my eyes, for my children,
but do not blind the Sun!   He is the father, the
provider — and how shall he watch against harm,
or how find us game without his bright eyes?
Blind me, and keep him all-seeing."

And the Trues said: "It is well, daughter."
And so they took away one of her eyes, so that
she could never see again so well.   Then night
came upon the tired earth, and the flowers and
birds and people slept their first sleep, and it was
very good.   But she who first had the love of
children, and paid for them with pain as mother's
pay, she did not grow ugly by her sacrifice.   Nay,

she is lovelier than ever, and we all love her to this day. For the Trues are good to her, and gave her in place of the bloom of girlhood the beauty that is only in the faces of mothers.

So mother-pale above us
She bends, her watch to keep,
Who of her sight dear-bought the night
To give her children sleep.

X

THE MAKER OF THE THUNDER-KNIVES

YOU have perhaps seen the beautiful arrow-heads of moss-agate, petrified wood, or volcanic glass which were used, until very recently, by the Indians of the Southwest, and are still treasured by them. At least you are familiar with the commoner flint ones left by the aboriginal tribes farther eastward. And seeing them, you must have wondered how they were ever made from such fearfully stubborn stone — always the very hardest that was accessible to the maker. I have tried for six hours, with the finest drills, to make a little hole in the thinnest part of an agate arrow-head, to put it on a charm-ring; but when the drill and I were completely worn out, there was not so much as a mark on the arrow-head to show what we had been doing. If you will take one to your jeweler, he will have as poor luck.

But the *making* of the arrow-heads is really a very simple matter; and I have fashioned many very fair ones. The only implements are part of a peculiarly shaped bone — preferably from the thigh of the elk — and a stick about the size of a lead-pencil, but of double the diameter. The maker of *puntas* takes the bone in his left hand; in his right is the stick, against which the selected splinter of stone is firmly pressed by the thumb.   With a firm, steady pressure against the sharp edge of the bone, a tiny flake is nicked from the splinter. Then the splinter is turned, and a nick is similarly made on the other side, just a little ahead of the first; and so on.   It is by this alternate nicking from opposite sides that the stone-splinter grows less by tiny flakes, and is shaped by degrees to a perfect arrow-head.   If you will notice the edge of an arrow-head, you will see plainly that the work was done in this way, for the edge is not a straight but a wavy line — sometimes even a zigzag, recalling the manner in which saw-teeth are "set."

Every Indian, and every one who has studied the Indian, knows this.   But if I ask one of my brown old *compadres* here, where he got the arrow-head which he wears as a charm about his wrinkled neck, he will not tell me any such story as that.   No, indeed!

Quáh-le-kee-raí-deh, the Horned Toad, gave it to him.   So?   Oh, yes!   He talked so nicely to a Horned Toad on the mesa [1] the other day, that the little creature put a *punta* where he could find it the next time he went thither.

Whenever a Pueblo sees a Quáh-le-kee-raí-deh, he jumps from his horse or his big farm-wagon, and makes every effort to capture the *animalito* before it can reach a hole.   If successful, he pulls from his blanket or his legging-garters a red thread — no other color will do — and ties it necklace-fashion

---

1 Table-land.

around the neck of his little prisoner. Then he
invokes all sorts of blessings on the Horned Toad,
assures it of his sincere respect and friendship,
begs it to remember him with a *punta*, and lets it
go. Next time he goes to the mesa, he fully ex-
pects to find an arrow-head, and generally *does*
find one—doubtless because he then searches
more carefully on that broad reach where so many
arrow-heads have been lost in ancient wars and
hunts. Finding one, he prays to the Sun-Father
and the Moon-Mother and all his other deities,
and returns profound thanks to the Horned Toad.
Some finders put the arrow-head in the pouch
which serves Indians for a pocket.[1] Some wear
it as an amulet on the necklace. In either case,
the belief is that no evil spirit can approach the
wearer while he has that charm about him. In
fact, it is a sovereign spell against witches.

The common belief of the Pueblos is that the
Horned Toad makes these arrow-heads only during
a storm, and deposits them at the very instant
when it thunders. For this reason an arrow-head
is always called *Kóh-un-shée-eh*, or thunder-knife.
The strange appearance of this quaint, spiked lizard
— which is really not a "hop-toad" at all—doubtless suggested the notion ; for his whole back is
covered with peculiar points which have very much
the shape and color of Indian arrow-heads.

Quáh-le-kee-raí-deh is a very important personage in the Pueblo folk-lore. He not only is the
inventor and patentee of the arrow-head and the

---

[1] The "left-hand-bag," *shur-taí-moo*, because it always hangs from the
right shoulder and under the left arm.

scalping-knife,[1] but he also invented irrigation, and taught it to man; and is a general benefactor of our race.

There is one very sacred folk-story which tells why boys must never smoke until they have proved their manhood. Pueblo etiquette is very strict on all such points.[2]

Once upon a time there lived in Isleta two boys who were cousins. One day their grandfather, who was a True Believer (in all the ancient rites), caught them in a corner smoking the *weer*. Greatly shocked, he said to them:

"Sons, I see you want to be men; but you must prove yourselves before you are thought to be. Know, then, that nobody is born with the freedom of the smoke, but every one must earn it. So go now, each of you, and bring me Quée-hla-kú-ee, the skin of the oak."

Now, in the talk of men, Quée-hla-kú-ee is another thing; but the boys did not know. They got their mothers to give them some tortillas,[3] and with this lunch they started for the Bosque (a 10,000-foot peak twenty miles east of Isleta). Reaching the mountain, they went to every kind of tree and cut a little piece of its bark — for they were not sure which was the oak. Then they came home, very tired, and carried the bark to their grandfather. But when he had looked at it all he said:

1 Which were formerly about the same thing — a large and sharp-edged arrow-head or similar stone being the only knife of the Pueblos in prehistoric times.

2 See my "Strange Corners of Our Country" (The Century Co.), chap. xviii.

3 A cake of unleavened batter cooked on a hot stone. They look something like a huge flapjack, but are very tough and keep a long time.

"Young men, you have not yet proved yourselves. So now it is for you to go again and look
for the *oak*-bark."

At this their hearts were heavy, but they took
tortillas and started again. On the way they met
an old Horned Toad, who stopped them and said:
"Young-men-friends, I know what trouble you
are in. Your *tata* has sent you for the skin of the
oak, but you do not know the oak he means. But
I will be the one to help you. Take these," and he
gave them two large thunder-knives, "and with
these in hand go up that cañon yonder. In a little
way you will see a great many of your enemies, the
Navajos, camping. On the first hill from which
you see their fire, there stop. In time, while you
wait there, you will hear a Coyote howling across
the cañon. Then is the time to give your enemy-
yell [war-whoop] and attack them."

The boys thanked the Horned Toad and went.
Presently they saw the camp-fire of the Navajos,
and waiting till the Coyote called they gave the
enemy-yell and then attacked. They had no weap-
ons except their thunder-knives, but with these they
killed several Navajos, and the others ran away.
In the dark and their hurry they made a mistake
and scalped a woman (which was never customary
with the Pueblos).

Taking their scalps, they hurried home to their
grandfather, and when he saw that they had
brought the real oak-skin (which is an Indian
euphemy for "scalp"), he led them proudly to the
Cacique, and the Cacique ordered the T'u-a-fú-ar
(scalp-dance). After the inside days, when the

takers of scalps must stay in the *estufa*, was the dance.   And when it came to the round dance at night the two boys were dancing side by side.

Then a young woman who was a stanger came and pushed them apart and danced between them. She was very handsome, and both fell in love with her.   But as soon as their hearts thought of love, a skeleton was between them in place of the girl — for they who go to war or take a scalp have no right to think of love.

They were very frightened, but kept dancing until they were too tired, and then went to the singers inside the circle to escape.   But the skeleton followed them and stood beside them, and they could not hide from it.

At last they began to run away, and went to the east.   Many moons they kept running, but the skeleton was always at their heels.   At last they came to the Sunrise Lake, wherein dwell the Trues of the East.

The guards let them in, and they told the Trues all that had happened, and the skeleton stood beside them.   The Trues said: "Young men, if you are men, sit down and we will protect you."

But when the boys looked again at the skeleton they could not stop, but ran away again.   Many moons they ran north till they came to where the Trues of the North dwell in the Black Lake of Tears.

The Trues of the North promised to defend them, but again the skeleton came and scared them away; and they ran for many moons until they came to the Trues of the West, who dwell

in T'hoor-kím-p'ah-whée-ay, the Yellow Lake
Where the Sun Sets. And there the same things
happened; and they ran away again to the south,
till they found the Trues of the South in P'ah-chéer-
p'ah-whée-ay, the Lake of Smooth Pebbles.

But there again it was the same, and again they
ran many moons till they came to the Trues of the
Center, who live here in Isleta. And here the
skeleton said to them:

"Why do you run from me now? For when
you were dancing you looked at me and loved me,
but now you run away."

But they could not answer her, and ran into the
room of the Trues of the Center, and told their
story. Then the Trues gave power to the Cum-
pa-huit-la-wid-deh[1] to see the skeleton,—which
no one else in the world could see, except the
Trues and the two young men,—and said to him:

"Shoot this person who follows these two."

So the Cum-pa-huit-la-wid-deh shot the skeleton through with an arrow from the left side to the
right side,[2] and took the scalp.

That was the end of the skeleton, and the young
men were free. And when the Trues had given
them counsel, they came to their people, and told
the Cacique all. He made a new scalp-dance, because they had not stayed to finish the first one.

And when the dance was done, they told all the
people what had happened. Then the principals
had a meeting and made a rule which is to this

---

[1] Guard at the door of the gods.
[2] The only official method of killing a witch, which is one of the chief
duties of the Cum-pa-huit-la-wen.

day, that in the twelve days of the scalp[1] no warrior shall think thoughts of love.

For it was because they had love-thoughts of the Navajo girl that her skeleton haunted them. And at the same time it was made the law, which still is, that no one shall smoke till he has taken a scalp to prove himself a man.

For if the boys had not been smoking when they had not freedom to, their grandfather would not have sent them, and all that trouble would not have come. And that is why.

[1] The period of fasting and purification before and during the scalp-dance.

XI

THE STONE-MOVING SONG

THE Horned Toad is also a famous musician— a sort of Pueblo Orpheus, whose song charms the very stones and trees. A short folk-story of Isleta refers to this.

One day Quáh-le-kee-raí-deh was working in his field. There were many very large rocks, and to move them he sang a strong song as he pulled:

> *Yah éh-ah, héh-ah háy-na,*
> *Yah, éh-ah, heh-ah hay-na,*
> *Wha-naí-kee-ay hee-e-wid-deh*
> *Ah-kwe-ée-hee ai-yén-cheh,*
> *Yahb-k'yáy-queer ah-chóo-hee.*

When he sang this and touched the heaviest stone, it rose up from the ground, and went over his head and fell far behind him.

While he worked so, Too-wháy-deh came along; and seeing what happened, he wished to meddle, as his way is. So he said:

"Friend Quáh-le-kee-raí-deh, let *me* do it."

"No, friend," said the Horned Toad. "It is better for every one to do what he knows, and not to put himself in the work of others."

"Do not think so," answered the Coyote. "For I can do this also. It is very easy."

"It is well, then — but see that you are not afraid; for so it will be bad."

Too-wháy-deh laid off his blanket and took hold of the largest rock there was, and sang the song. When he sang, the rock rose up in the air to go over his head; but he, being scared, ducked his head. Then at once the rock fell on him, and he had no bones left. Then the Horned Toad laughed, and gave the enemy-yell (war-whoop), saying: "We do this to one another!"

XII

THE COYOTE AND THE THUNDER-KNIFE

ANOTHER Isleta myth tells of an equally sad misadventure of the Coyote.

Once upon a time an old Coyote-father took a walk away from home; for in that season of the year his babies were so peevish they would not let him sleep. It happened that a Locust was making pottery, under a tree; and every time she moved the molding-spoon around the soft clay jar, she sang a song. The Coyote, coming near and hearing, thought: "Now that is the very song I need to put my *óo-un* to sleep." And following the sound he came to the tree, and found Cheech-wée-deh at work. But she had stopped singing.

"Locust-friend," said he, "come teach me that song, so that I can soothe my children to sleep." But the Locust did not move to answer; and he repeated:

"Locust-friend, come teach me that song."

Still she did not answer, and the Coyote, losing his patience, said:

"Locust, if you don't teach me that song, I will eat you up!"

At that, the Locust showed him the song, and he sang with her until he knew how.

"Now I know it, thank you," he said. "So I will go home and sing it to my children, and they will sleep."

So he went. But as he came to a pool, half-way home, a flock of Afraids-of-the-Water [1] flew up at his very nose, and drove out his memory. He went looking around, turning over the stones and peeping in the grass; but he could not find the song anywhere. So he started back at last to get the Locust to teach him again.

But while he was yet far, the Locust saw him, so she shed her skin, leaving a dry husk, as snakes do, and filled it with sand. Then she made it to sit up, and put the molding-spoon in its hands, and the clay jars in front of it; and she herself flew up into the tree.

Coming, the Coyote said: "Friend Locust, show that song again; for I got scared, and the song was driven out of me." But there was no answer.

"Hear, Locust! I will ask just once more; and if you do not show me the song, I'll swallow you!"

Still she did not reply; and the Coyote, being angry, swallowed the stuffed skin, sand, spoon, and all, and started homeward, saying: "*Now* I think I have that song in me!"

But when he was half-way home he stopped and struck himself, and said: "What a fool, truly! For now I am going home without a song. But if I had left the Locust alive, and bothered her long enough, she would have shown me. I think now

1 The ironical Tée-wahn name for ducks.

I will take her out, to see if she will not sing for me."

So he ran all around, hunting for a black thunder-knife,[1] and singing:

Where can I find Shée-eh-fóon ?
Where can I find Shée-eh-fóon ?

At last he found a large piece of the black-rock, and broke it until he got a knife. He made a mark on his breast with his finger, saying: " Here I will cut, and take her out."

Then he cut. " Mercy!" said he, "but it bites!" He cut again, harder. "Goodness! but how it bites!" he cried, very loud. And cutting a third time, he fell down and died. So he did not learn the song of the pottery-making.

The Quères Pueblos have exactly the same folk-story, except that they make the Horned Toad, instead of the Locust, the music-teacher. In their version, the Horned Toad, after being swallowed, kills the Coyote by lifting its spines. Remembering what I have said of the maker of the thunder-knives, you will readily see the analogy between this and the obsidian splinter of the Tée-wahn story. It is, indeed, one of the most characteristic and instructive examples of the manner in which a folk-story becomes changed.

[1] One of obsidian, or volcanic glass.

XIII

I FANCY I must have been dozing after that hard ride; for when a far-away, cracked voice that could be none other than Grandfather Ysidro's said, *"Kah-whee-cá-me, Lorenso-kaí-deh!"* I started up so hastily as to bump my head against the whitewashed wall. That may seem a queer sentence to rouse one so sharply; and especially when you know what it means. It meant that old Ysidro[1] had just finished a story, which I had altogether missed, and was now calling upon the old man next him to tell one, by using the customary Pueblo saying:

"There is a tail to you, Father Lorenso!"

[1] Pronounced Ee-seé-droh.

Kah-whee-cá-me is what a Tée-wahn Indian always says in such a case, instead of " Now *you* tell
a story, friend." It is not intended as an impolite
remark, but merely refers to the firm belief of these
quaint people that if one were to act like a stubborn donkey, and refuse to tell a story when called
on, a donkey's tail would grow upon him!

With such a fate in prospect, you may be sure
that the roundabout invitation thus conveyed is
never declined.

Grandfather Lorenso bows his head gravely,
but seems in no haste. He is indeed impressively
deliberate as he slowly makes a cigarette from a
bit of corn-husk and a pinch of tobacco, lights it
upon a coal raked out of the fireplace by his
withered fingers, blows a slow puff eastward, then
one to the north, another to the west, a fourth to
the south, one straight above his head, and one
down toward the floor. There is one part of the
United States where the compass has *six* cardinal
points (those I have just named), and that is among
these Indians, and in fact all the others of the
Southwest. The cigarette plays a really important part in many sacred ceremonies of the
Pueblos; for, as I have explained, its collective
smoke is thought to be what makes the rain-
clouds and brings the rain; and it is also a charm
against witches.

Having thus propitiated the divinities who dwell
in the directions named, Lorenso looks about the
circle to see if all are listening. The glance satis-
fies him — as well it may. There are no heedless
eyes or ears in the audience, of which I am the

only white member — and a very lucky one, in that I, an "Americano," am allowed to hear these jealously guarded stories, and to see the silent smoke-prayer which would never be made if a stranger were present. There are seven agèd men here, and nine bright-eyed boys — all *Isleteños* (inhabitants of Isleta). We are huddled around the fireplace in the corner of the big, pleasant room, against whose dark rafters and farther white walls the shadows dance and waver.

And now, taking a deep puff, Lorenso exclaims: *"Nah-t' hóo-ai!"* (In a house.) It has nothing to do with the story; but is the prologue to inform the hearers that the story is about to open.

"Ah-h-h!" we all responded, which is as much as to say, "We are listening — go on"; and Lorenso begins his story.

Once upon a time there was a Tée-wahn village on the other side of the mountain, and there lived a man and his wife who thought more of the future of their children than did the others. To care better for the children they moved to a little ranch some distance from the village, and there taught their two little sons all they could. Both boys loved the outdoors, and games, and hunting; and the parents were well pleased, saying to each other:

"Perhaps some day they will be great hunters!"

By the time the elder boy was twelve and the younger ten, they both were very expert with the little bows and arrows their father carefully made them; and already they began to bring home many rabbits when they were allowed to go a little way from home. There was only one command their parents gave about their hunts; and that was that they must never, never go south. They could hunt to the east, north, and west, but not south.

Day after day they went hunting, and more and more rabbits they killed, growing always more expert.

One day when they had hunted eastward, the elder boy said:

"Brother, can you say any reason why we must not go south?"

"I know nothing," replied the younger, "except what I overheard our parents saying one day. They spoke of an old woman who lives in the south who eats children; and for that they said they would never let us go south."

"Pooh!" said the elder, "I think nothing of *that*. The real reason must be that they wish to save the rabbits in the south, and are afraid we would kill them all. There must be many rabbits in that *bosque* [forest] away down there. Let's go and see — *they* won't know!"

The younger boy being persuaded, they started off together, and after a long walk came to the *bosque*. It was full of rabbits, and they were having great sport, when suddenly they heard a motherly voice calling through the woods. In a moment they saw an old woman coming from the south, who said to the boys:

"*Mah-kóo-oon* [grandchildren], what are you doing here, where no one ever thinks to come?"

"We are hunting, Grandmother," they replied. 'Our parents would never let us come south; but

to-day we came to see if the rabbits are more numerous here than above."

"Oh!" said the old woman, "this game you see
here is *nothing*.   Come, and I will show you where
there is much, and you can carry very large rabbits home to your parents."   But she was deceiv-
ing them.

She had a big basket upon her back, and stooping for the boys to get into it, she carried them
farther and farther into the woods.   At last they
came to an old, battered house; and setting the
basket down, she said :

"Now we have come all the way here, where no
one ever came before, and there is no way out.
You can find no trail, and you will have to stay
here contented, or I will eat you up!"

The boys were much afraid, and said they would
stay and be contented.   But the old woman went
into the house and told her husband—who was as
wicked as she—to get wood and build a big fire
in the *horno*.[1]   All day long the fire burned, and
the oven became hotter than it had ever been.   In
the evening the old witch-woman raked out the
coals, and calling the boys seized them and forced
them into the fiery oven.

"*Tahb-kóon-nahm?*" (Is that so?) we all ex-
claimed—that being the proper response whenever
the narrator pauses a moment.

"That is so," replied Lorenso, and went on.

Then the old woman put a flat rock over the
little door of the oven, and another over the smoke-

_____
1 An outdoor bake-oven, made of clay, and shaped like a beehive.

hole, and sealed them both tight with clay. All that night she and her husband were chuckling to think what a nice breakfast they would have — for both of them were witch-people, and ate all the children they could find.

But in the morning when she unsealed the oven, there were the two boys, laughing and playing together unhurt — for the Wháy-nin [1] had come to their aid and protected them from the heat.

Leaving the boys to crawl out, the old woman ran to the house and scolded the old man terribly for not having made the oven hot enough. "Go this minute," she said, "and put in the oven all the wood that it will hold, and keep it burning all day!"

When night came, the old woman cleaned the oven, which was twice as hot as before ; and again she put in the boys and sealed it up. But the next morning the boys were unhurt and went to playing.

The witch-woman was very angry then ; and giving the boys their bows and arrows, told them to go and play. She stayed at home and abused the old witch-man all day for a poor fire-maker.

When the boys returned in the evening, she said:

"To-morrow, grandchildren, we will play *Nah-oo-p'ah-chée* (hide-and-seek), and the one who is found three times by the other shall pay his life."

The boys agreed,[2] and secretly prayed to the Trues to help them — for by this time they knew that the old man and the old woman "had the bad road."

[1] "The Trues," as the Pueblos call their highest divinities.
[2] For such a challenge, which was once a common one with the Indians, could not possibly be declined.

The next day came; and very soon the old woman called them to begin the game. The boys were to hide first; and when the old woman had turned her eyes and vowed not to look, they went to the door and hid, one against each of its jambs. There you could look and look, and see the wood through them—for the Trues, to help them, made them invisible. When they were safely hidden they whooped, *"Hee-táh!"* and the old woman began to hunt, singing the hide-and-seek song:

Hee-táh yahn
Hee choo-ah-kóo
Mee, mee, mee ?

(Now, now,
Which way
Went they, went they, went they?)

After hunting some time she called:

"You little fellows are on the door-posts. Come out!"

So the boys came out and "made blind" (covered their eyes) while the old woman went to hide. There was a pond close by, with many ducks on it; and making herself very little, she went and hid under the left wing of the duck with a blue head.[1]

When they heard her "*Hee-táh!*" the boys went searching and singing; and at last the elder cried out:

" Old woman, you are under the left wing of the whitest duck on the lake — the one with the blue head. Come out!"

This time the boys made themselves small and crawled into the quivers beside their bows and arrows. The old woman had to sing her song over a great many times, as she went hunting all around; but at last she called:

"Come out of the quivers where you are!"

Then the witch made herself very small indeed, and went behind the foot of a big crane that was standing on one leg near the lake. But at last the boys found her even there.

It was their last turn now, and the old woman felt very triumphant as she waited for them to hide. But this time they went up and hid themselves under the right arm of the Sun.[2] The old witch hunted everywhere, and used all her bad power, but in vain; and when she was tired out she had

---

[1] I should tell you that, being a witch, she could not possibly have gone under the right wing. Everything that is to the left belongs to the witches.
[2] Who is, in the Pueblo belief, the father of all things.

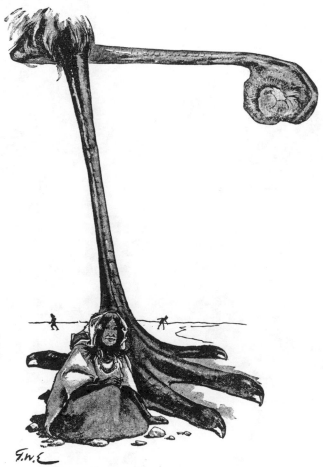

"THE WITCH MADE HERSELF VERY SMALL, AND WENT
BEHIND THE FOOT OF A BIG CRANE."

to cry, "*Hee-táh-ow!*" And then the boys came down from under the Sun's arm rejoicing.

The old witch, taking her last turn, went to the lake and entered into a fish, thinking that there she would be perfectly safe from discovery. It did take the boys a great while to find her; but at last they shouted:

"Old woman, you are in the biggest fish in the lake. Come out!"

As she came walking toward them in her natural shape again, they called: "Remember the agreement!" and with their sharp arrows they killed the old witch-woman and then the old witch-man. Then they took away the two wicked old hearts, and put in place of each a kernel of spotless corn; so that if the witches should ever come to life again they would no longer be witches, but people with pure, good hearts. They never did come to life, however, which was just as well.

Taking their bows and arrows, the boys — now young men, for the four "days" they had been with the witches were really four years — returned home. At the village they found their anxious parents, who had come to ask the Cacique to order all the people out to search.

When all saw the boys and heard their story, there was great rejoicing, for those two witch-people had been terrors to the village for years. On their account no one had dared go hunting to the south. And to this day the game is thicker there than anywhere else in the country, because it has not been hunted there for so long as in other places. The two young men were forgiven for disobedience (which is a very serious thing at any age, among the Pueblos), and were made heroes. The Cacique gave them his two daughters for wives, and all the people did them honor.[1]

"Is that so?" we responded; and Lorenso replied, "That is so," gathering his blanket and rising to go without "putting a tail" to any one, for it was already late.

I may add that the game of hide-and-seek is still played by my dusky little neighbors, the Pueblo children, and the searching-song is still sung by them, exactly as the boys and the old witch played and sang — but of course without their magical talent at hiding.

[1] This story seems to be one of the myths about the Hero Twin Brothers, the children of the Sun. They are, next to Sun-Father and Moon-Mother, the chief deities of all the southwestern tribes. In the Quères folk-lore they figure very prominently; but in the Tée-wahn are more disguised.

XIV

THE RACE OF THE TAILS

NEARLY every people has its own version of
the race of the Hare and the Tortoise. That
current among the Pueblos makes the Rabbit the
hero, by a trick rather cleverer than Æsop's.

Once the Coyote came where Pee-oo-ée-deh,
the little "cotton-tail" rabbit, sat at the door of
his house, thinking.

"What do you think, friend Pee-oo-ée-deh?"
said the Coyote.

"I am thinking, friend Too-whāy-deh, why some
have large tails like you; but we have no tails.
Perhaps if we had tails like yours, we could run
straight; but now we have to hop."

"It is true, *ah-bóo*,"[1] said the Coyote, not knowing that the Rabbit laughed in his heart. "For I
can run faster than any one, and never did any
gain from me in the foot-races. But *you,*—you just
hop like a bird."

The Rabbit made a sad face, and the Coyote
said: "But come, friend Pee-oo-ée-deh, let us run
a race. We will run around the world, and see

[1] Poor thing.

who will win.   And whichever shall come in first,
he shall kill the other and eat him."[1]

"It is well," answered the Rabbit.   "In four
days we will run."

Then the Coyote went home very glad.   But
Pee-oo-ée-deh called a *junta* of all his tribe, and
told them how it was, and the way he thought to
win the race.   And when they had heard, they all
said: "It is well.   Fear not, for we will be the ones
that will help you."

When the fourth day came, the Coyote arrived
smiling, and threw down his blanket, and stood
ready in only the dark blue *taparabo*,[2] saying:
"But what is the use to run?   For I shall win.   It
is better that I eat you now, before you are tired."

But the Rabbit threw off his blanket, and tight-
ened his *taparabo*, and said: "Pooh!   For the end
of the race is far away, and *there* is time to talk of
eating.   Come, we will run around the four sides
of the world.[3]   But *I* shall run underground, for
so it is easier for me."

Then they stood up side by side.   And when
they were ready, the Capitan shouted "*Haí-koo!*"
and they ran.   The Coyote ran with all his legs;
but the Rabbit jumped into his hole and threw out
sand, as those who dig very fast.

Now for many days the Coyote kept running to
the east, and saw nothing of Pee-oo-ée-deh.   But

1 A challenge of this sort, with life as the stake, was very common
among all Indians; and it was impossible for the challenged to decline. This
story recalls that of the Antelope Boy.   Four days always elapsed between
the challenge and the race.

2 Breech-clout, which is the only thing worn in a foot-race.

3 Which the Pueblos believe to be flat and square.

just as he came to the east and was turning to the
north, up jumped a rabbit from under the ground
in front of him, and shouted: "We do this to one
another"; and jumped back in the hole and began
to throw out dirt very hard.

"Ai!" said the Coyote. "I wish I could run
under the ground like that, for it seems very easy.
For all these days I have run faster than ever any
one ran; yet Pee-oo-ée-deh comes to the east
ahead of me." But he did not know it was the
brother of Pee-oo-ée-deh, who had come out to
the east to wait for him.

So Too-whây-deh ran harder; and after many
days he came to the end of the world, to the
north. But just as he was to turn west, up
sprang a rabbit in front of him, and taunted him,
and went back in its hole, digging.

The Coyote's heart was heavy, but he ran *very*
hard. "Surely," he said, "no one can run so fast
as *this*."

But when he came to the west, a rabbit sprang
up ahead of him, and mocked him, and went again
under the ground. And when he had run to the
south, there was the same thing. At last, very
tired and with his tongue out, he came in sight of
the starting-point, and there was Pee-oo-ée-deh,
sitting at the door of his house, smoothing his hair.
And he said: "Pooh! Coyote-friend, we do this to
one another. For now it is clear that big tails are
not good to run with, since I have been waiting
here a long time for you. Come here, then, that I
may eat you, though you are tough."

But Too-whây-deh, being a coward, ran away and

would not pay his bet. And all the brothers of Pee-oo-ée-deh laughed for the trick they had put upon the Coyote.

In a case which I knew of, years ago, this folk-story seems to have given a hint to human racers. A Mexican who owned a large and very fleet-footed burro, challenged a young Indian of Acoma to a ten-mile race. The Indian was a very famous runner, and the challenger depended on the distance alone to wear him out. In accordance with the conditions the rivals started together from the goal, the Indian on foot, the Mexican on his burro. For about four miles the Indian left the galloping donkey far behind; but he could not keep up such a tremendous pace, and the burro began to gain. About midway of the course where the trail touches a great lava-flow, the Indian dove into a cave. Just as the Mexican was passing, out came an Indian, passed the burro with a magnificent spurt, and after a long run reached the farther goal about a hundred feet ahead. Unfortunately for him, however, the trick was detected — he was the twin brother of the challenged man, and had awaited him in the cave, taking up the race fresh when the first runner was tired!

XV

HONEST BIG-EARS

NEARLY all of you have seen pictures of the Burro, the quaint little donkey of the South-west. He is very small,— not more than half the weight of a smallish mule,— but very strong, very sure-footed, and very reliable. And he is one of the drollest, "cutest," wisest-looking creatures on earth.

T'ah-hlá-a-hloon, or Big-ears, as the Tée-wahn call him, does not appear very often in their folk-lore — and for a very natural reason. Most of these myths were made centuries before a white man ever saw this country; and until Europeans came, there were neither horses, donkeys, sheep, goats, cats, nor cattle (except the buffalo) in either America. It was the Spanish pioneers who gave all these animals to the Pueblos. Nor did the Indians have milk, cheese, wheat, or metals of any sort. So when we see a story in which any of these things are mentioned, we may know that it was made within the last three hundred and fifty years — or that an old story has been modified to include them.

There is one of these comparatively modern

nursery-tales which is designed to show the honesty and wisdom of the Burro.

Once Big-ears was coming alone from the farm of his master to Isleta, carrying a load of curd cheeses done up in buckskin bags. As he came through the hills he met a Coyote, who said:

"Friend Big-ears, what do you carry on your back?"

"I carry many cheeses for my master, friend Too-wháy-deh," answered the Burro.

"Then give me one, friend, for I am hunger-dying."

"No," said the Burro, "I cannot give you one, for my master would blame me — since they are not mine but his, and a man of the pueblo waits for them."

Many times the Coyote asked him, with soft words; but Big-ears would not, and went his way. Then Too-wháy-deh followed him behind, without noise, and slyly bit the bag and stole a cheese. But Big-ears did not know it, for he could not see behind.

When he came to the pueblo, the man who awaited him unloaded the cheeses and counted them. "There lacks one," he said; "for thy master said he would send *so* many. Where is the other?"

"Truly, I know not," answered Big-ears, "but I think Too-wháy-deh stole it; for he asked me on the way to give him a cheese. But wait — I will pay him!"

So Big-ears went back to the hills and looked for the house of Too-wháy-deh. At last he found it, but the Coyote was nowhere. So he lay down near the hole, and stretched his legs out as if dead, and opened his mouth wide, and was very still.

Time passing so, the Old-Woman-Coyote came out of the house to bring a jar of water. But when she saw the Burro lying there, she dropped her *tinaja*, and ran in crying:

"*Hloo-hli!*[1] come out and see! For a *buffalo* has died out here, and we must take in some meat."

So Old-Man-Coyote came out, and was very glad, and began to sharpen his knife.

But his wife said: "But before you cut him up, get me the liver, for I am very hungry"—and the liver is that which all the foxes like best.

Then the Old-Man-Coyote, thinking to please her, went into the Burro's mouth to get the liver; but Big-ears shut his teeth on Too-wháy-deh's head, and jumped up and ran home. The Old-Woman-Coyote followed running, crying: "*Ay, Nana!* Let go!" But Big-ears would not listen to her, and brought the thief to his master. When the master heard what had been, he killed the Coyote, and thanked Big-ears, and gave him much grass. And this is why, ever since, Big-ears strikes with his hind feet if anything comes behind him slyly; for he remembers how Too-wháy-deh stole the cheese.

1 Old Man.

XVI

THE FEATHERED BARBERS

THE Coyote, one summer day, having taken a bath in the river, lay down in the hot sand to dry himself. While he was sleeping there, a crowd of Quails came along; and seeing that he was asleep, they said:

"Huh! Here is that foolish Too-whây-deh. Let us give him a trick!"

So they cut off all his hair, which makes one to be laughed at, and ran away.

When the Coyote woke up he was ashamed, and wished to punish those who had made him *pelado;* and he ran around to see if he could find the tracks of an enemy. There were only the tracks of the Quails, so he knew they had done it. Very angry, he followed the trail until it went into a large hole. He went all around to see if they had not come out; but there were no other tracks, so he went in. First the hole was big, but then it grew small, and he had to dig. When he had dug a long time, he caught a Quail, and he said:

"Ho, Ch'um-níd-deh! It is you that cut my hair and left me a laughed-at. But I am going to eat you this very now!"

"No, friend Too-wháy-deh, it was another who did it. You will find him farther in, with the scissors[1] still in his hand."

So the Coyote let that Quail go, and dug and dug till he caught another. But that one said the same thing; and Too-wháy-deh let him go, and dug after the next one. So it was, until he had let them all go, one by one; and when he came to the very end of the hole, there were no more.

With this, the Coyote was very angry, and ran out of the hole, promising to catch and eat them all. As he came out he met the Cotton-tail, and cried with a fierce face:

"Hear, you Pee-oo-ée-deh! If you don't catch me the Ch'úm-nin that cut my hair, I 'll eat *you!*"

"Oh, I can catch them, friend Coyote," said the Rabbit. "See, here is their trail!"

When they had followed the trail a long way, they saw the birds sitting and laughing under a bush.

"Now you wait here while I go and catch them," said Pee-oo-ée-deh. So the Coyote sat down to rest. As soon as the Rabbit was near them, the Quails flew a little way, and he kept running after them. But as soon as they were over a little hill, he turned aside and ran home, and the Coyote never knew if the Quails were caught or not.

1 This indicates that the tale is comparatively modern.

THE ACCURSED LAKE

XVII

AWAY to the southeast of the Manzano Mountains, two days' journey from my pueblo of Isleta, are the shallow salt lakes. For scores of miles their dazzling sheen is visible — a strange patch of silver on the vast brown plains. They are near the noblest ruins in our North America—the wondrous piles of massive masonry of Abó, Cuaray, and the so-called "Gran Quivira"—the latter the home of the silliest delusion that ever lured treasure-hunters to their death. The whole region has a romantic history, and is important to the scientific student. From that locality

came, centuries ago, part of the people who then
founded Isleta, and whose descendants dwell here
to this day. Perhaps you would like to know *why*
those lakes are salt now — for my Indian neighbors
say that once they were fresh and full of fish, and
that the deer and buffalo came from all the country
round to drink there. The story is very important
ethnologically, for it tells much of the strange secret religion of the Pueblos, and more concerning
the, method of initiating a young Indian into one
of the orders of medicine-men — both matters which
men of science have found extremely difficult to
be learned. Here is the story as it is believed by
the Tée-wahn, and as it was related to me by one
of them.

Long ago there was still a village east of Shoo-
paht-hóo-eh, the Eagle-Feather (Manzano) Mountains, and in it lived a famous hunter. One day,
going out on the plains to the east, he stalked a
herd of antelopes, and wounded one with his arrows. It fled eastward, while the herd went south;
and the hunter began to trail it by the drops of
blood. Presently he came to the largest lake, into
which the trail led. As he stood on the bank, wondering what to do, a fish thrust its head from the
water and said:
"Friend Hunter, you are on dangerous ground!"
and off it went swimming. Before the Hunter
could recover from his surprise, a Lake-Man came
up out of the water and said:
"How is it that you are here, where no human
ever came?"

The Hunter told his story, and the Lake-Man invited him to come in. When he had entered the lake, he came to a house with doors to the east, north, west, and south, and a trap-door in the roof, with a ladder; and by the latter door they entered. In their talk together the Lake-Man learned that the Hunter had a wife and little son at home.

"If that is so," said he, "why do you not come and live with me? I am here alone, and have plenty of other food, but I am no hunter. We could live very well here together." And opening doors on four sides of the room he showed the Hunter four other huge rooms, all piled from floor to ceiling with corn and wheat and dried squash and the like.

"That is a very good offer," said the astonished Hunter. "I will come again in four days; and if my Cacique will let me, I will bring my family and stay."

So the Hunter went home—killing an antelope on the way—and told his wife all. She thought very well of the offer; and he went to ask permission of the Cacique. The Cacique demurred, for this was the best hunter in all the pueblo,[1] but at last consented and gave him his blessing.

So on the fourth day the Hunter and his wife and little boy came to the lake with all their property. The Lake-Man met them cordially, and gave the house and all its contents into the charge of the woman.[2]

Some time passed very pleasantly, the Hunter going out daily and bringing back great quantities

---

[1] All hunters give the Cacique a tenth of their game, for his support.
[2] As is the custom among all Pueblo Indians.

THE HUNTER AND THE LAKE-MAN.

of game. At last the Lake-Man, who was of an evil heart, pretended to show the Hunter something in the east room; and pushing him in, locked the great door and left him there to starve—for the room was full of the bones of men whom he had already entrapped in the same way.

The boy was now big enough to use his bow and arrows so well that he brought home many rabbits; and the witch-hearted Lake-Man began to plot to get him, too, out of the way.

So one morning when the boy was about to start for a hunt, he heard his mother groaning as if about to die; and the Lake-Man said to him:

"My boy, your mother has a terrible pain, and the only thing that will cure her is some ice from T'hoor-p'ah-whée-ai [Lake of the Sun],[1] the water from which the sun rises."

"Then," said the boy, straightway, "if that is so, I will take the heart of a man [that is, be brave] and go and get the ice for my little mother." And away he started toward the unknown east.

Far out over the endless brown plains he trudged bravely; until at last he came to the house of Shee-chóo-hlee-oh, the Old-Woman-Mole, who was there all alone—for her husband had gone to hunt. They were dreadfully poor, and the house was almost falling down, and the poor, wrinkled Old-Woman-Mole sat huddled in the corner by the fireplace, trying to keep warm by a few dying coals. But when the boy knocked, she rose and welcomed him kindly and gave him all there was in the house to eat—a wee bowl of soup with a

8   [1] Located "somewhere to the east"; perhaps the ocean.

patched-up snowbird in it.   The boy was very
hungry, and picking up the snowbird bit a big
piece out of it.

"Oh, my child!" cried the old woman, beginning
to weep. "You have ruined me! For my husband
trapped that bird these many years ago, but we
could never get another; and that is all we have
had to eat ever since.   So we never bit it, but
cooked it over and over and drank the broth. And
now not even that is left."   And she wept bitterly.

"Nay, Grandmother, do not worry," said the
boy.   "Have you any long hairs?"—for he saw
many snowbirds lighting near by.

"No, my child," said the old woman sadly.
"There is no other living animal here, and you
are the first human that ever came here."

But the boy pulled out some of his own long
hair and made snares, and soon caught many birds.
Then the Old-Woman-Mole was full of joy; and
having learned his errand, she said:

"My son, fear not, for I will be the one that shall
help you.   When you come into the house of the
Trues, they will tempt you with a seat; but you
must sit down only on what you have.[1]   Then they
will try you with smoking the *weer*, but I will help you."

Then she gave him her blessing, and the boy
started away to the east.   At last, after a weary,
weary way, he came so near the Sun Lake, that
the *Whit-lah-wíd-deh*[2] of the Trues saw him coming, and went in to report.

[1] That is, upon his blanket and moccasins, the unvarying etiquette of the
Medicine House.

[2] One of an order of medicine-men, who among other duties, act as guards
of the Medicine House.

"Let him be brought in," said the Trues; and the Whit-lah-wíd-deh took the boy in and in through eight rooms, until he stood in the presence of all the gods, in a vast room. There were all the gods of the East, whose color is white, and the blue gods of the North, the yellow gods of the West, the red gods of the South, and the rainbow-colored gods of the Up, the Down, and the Center, all in human shape. Beyond their seats were all the sacred animals — the buffalo, the bear, the eagle, the badger, the mountain lion, the rattlesnake, and all the others that are powerful in medicine.

Then the Trues bade the boy sit down, and offered him a white *manta* (robe) for a seat; but he declined respectfully, saying that he had been taught, when in the presence of his elders, to sit on nothing save what he brought, and he sat upon his blanket and moccasins. When he had told his story, the Trues tried him, and gave him the sacred *weer* to smoke—a hollow reed rammed with *pee-en-hleh*.[1] He smoked, and held the smoke bravely. But just then the Old-Woman-Mole, who had followed him underground all this way, dug a hole up to his very toes; and the smoke went down through his feet into the hole, and away back to the Old-Woman-Mole's house, where it poured out in a great cloud. And not the tiniest particle escaped into the room of the Trues. He finished the second *weer*[2] without being sick at all; and the

---

[1] The smoking of the pungent *weer* is a very severe ordeal; and it is a disgrace to let any of the smoke escape from the mouth or nose.

[2] Two being the usual number given a candidate for initiation into a medicine order.

Trues said, "Yes, he is our son.   But we will try him once more."   So they put him into the room of the East with the bear and the lion; and the savage animals came forward and breathed on him, but would not hurt him.   Then they put him into the room of the North, with the eagle and the hawk; then into the room of the West, with the snakes; and lastly, into the room of the South, where were the Apaches and all the other human enemies of his people.   And from each room he came forth unscratched.

"Surely," said the Trues, "this is our son! But once more we will try him."

They had a great pile of logs built up ("cob-house" fashion), and the space between filled with pine-knots.   Then the Whit-lah-wíd-deh set the boy on the top of the pile and lighted it.

But in the morning, when the guard went out, there was the boy unharmed and saying: "Tell the Trues I am cold, and would like more fire."

Then he was brought again before the Trues, who said: "Son, you have proved yourself a True Believer, and now you shall have what you seek."

So the sacred ice was given him, and he started homeward — stopping on the way only to thank the Old-Woman-Mole, to whose aid he owed his success.

When the wicked Lake-Man saw the boy coming, he was very angry, for he had never expected him to return from that dangerous mission.   But he deceived the boy and the woman; and in a few days made a similar excuse to send the boy to the gods of the South after more ice for his mother.

The boy started off as bravely as before. When he had traveled a great way to the south, he came to a drying lake; and there, dying in the mud, was a little fish.

"*Ah-bóo* [poor thing], little fish," said the boy; and picking it up, he put it in his gourd canteen of water. After awhile he came to a good lake; and as he sat down to eat his lunch the fish in his gourd said:

"Friend Boy, let me swim while you eat, for I love the water."

So he put the fish in the lake; and when he was ready to go on, the fish came to him, and he put it back in his gourd. At three lakes he let the fish swim while he ate; and each time the fish came back to him. But beyond the third lake began a great forest which stretched clear across the world, and was so dense with thorns and brush that no man could pass it. But as the boy was wondering what he should do, the tiny fish changed itself into a great Fish-Animal with a very hard, strong skin,[1] and bidding the boy mount upon its back, it went plowing through the forest, breaking down big trees like stubble, and bringing him through to the other side without a scratch.

"Now, Friend Boy," said the Fish-Animal, "you saved my life, and I will be the one that shall help you. When you come to the house

1 It is quite possible that this "Fish-Animal with a hard, strong skin," living far to the south, is the alligator. Of course, the Pueblos never saw that strange saurian; but they probably heard of it in the earliest days from nomad tribes, and as a great scientist has pointed out, we may always depend upon it that there is a nucleus of truth in all these folk-myths. Such a strange animal, once heard of, would be very sure to figure in some story.

of the Trues, they will try you as they did in the East. And when you have proved yourself, the Cacique will bring you his three daughters, from whom to choose you a wife. The two eldest are very beautiful, and the youngest is not; but you ought to choose her, for beauty does not always reach to the heart."

The boy thanked his fish-friend and went on, until at last he came to the house of the Trues of the South. There they tried him with the *weer* and the fire, just as the Trues of the East had done, but he proved himself a man, and they gave him the ice. Then the Cacique brought his three daughters, and said:

"Son, you are now old enough to have a wife,[1] and I see that you are a true man who will dare all for his mother. Choose, therefore, one of my daughters."

The boy looked at the three girls; and truly the eldest were very lovely. But he remembered the words of his fish friend, and said:

"Let the youngest be my wife."

Then the Cacique was pleased, for he loved this daughter more than both the others. And the boy and the Cacique's daughter were married and started homeward, carrying the ice and many presents.

When they came to the great forest, there was the Fish-Animal waiting for them, and taking both on his back he carried them safely through. At the first lake he bade them good-by and blessed them, and they trudged on alone.

[1] For it must be remembered that all these travels had taken many years.

THE CURSING OF THE LAKE.

At last they came in sight of the big lake, and over it were great clouds, with the forked lightning leaping forth. While they were yet far off, they could see the wicked Lake-Man sitting at the top of his ladder, watching to see if the boy would return, and even while they looked they saw the lightning of the Trues strike him and tear him to shreds.

When they came to the lake the boy found his mother weeping for him as dead. And taking his wife and his mother,—but none of the things of the Lake-Man, for those were bewitched,—the boy came out upon the shore. There he stood and prayed to the Trues that the lake might be accurst forever; and they heard his prayer, for from that day its waters turned salt, and no living thing has drunk therefrom.

XVIII

THE MOQUI[1] BOY AND THE EAGLE

SOME of the folk-stories told in Isleta were evidently invented in other pueblos, whence the Tée-wahn have learned them in their trading-trips. There is even a story from the far-off towns of Moqui, three hundred miles west of here and ninety miles from the railroad. The Moquis live in northeast Arizona, in strange adobe towns,[2] perched upon impregnable islands of rock, rising far above the bare, brown plain. They are seldom visited and little known by white men. All the other Pueblo towns and tribes have changed somewhat in the present era of American occupation; but the Moquis remain very much as they were when the first Spaniard found them — three hundred and fifty years ago. They retain many customs long extinct among their kindred, and have some of which no trace is to be found elsewhere. One of the minor differences, but one which would be almost the first to strike a stranger, is the absence of captive eagles in Moqui; and this is explained by the following folk-story :

[1] Pronounced Móh-kee.
[2] See " Some Strange Corners of Our Country." The Century Co., New York.

The Eagle is Kah-báy-deh (commander) of all that flies, and his feathers are strongest in medicine.

So long ago that no man can tell how long, there lived in Moqui an old man and an old woman, who had two children — a boy and a girl. The boy, whose name was Tái-oh, had a pet Eagle, of which he was very fond; and the Eagle loved its young master. Despite his youth, Tái-oh was a capital hunter; and every day he brought home not only rabbits enough for the family, but also to keep the Eagle well fed.

One day when he was about to start on a hunt, he asked his sister to look out for the Eagle during his absence. No sooner was he out of sight than the girl began to upbraid the bird bitterly, saying: "How I hate you, for my brother loves you so much. If it were not for you, he would give me many more rabbits, but now you eat them up."

The Eagle, feeling the injustice of this, was angry; so when she brought him a rabbit for breakfast the Eagle turned his head and looked at it sidewise, and would not touch it. At noon, when she brought him his dinner, he did the same thing; and at night, when Tái-oh returned, the Eagle told him all that had happened.

"Now," said the Eagle, "I am very tired of staying always here in Moqui, and I want to go home to visit my people a little. Come and go along with me, that you may see where the Eagle-people live."

"It is well," replied Tái-oh. "To-morrow morning we will go together."

In the morning they all went out into the fields, far down in the valley, to hoe their corn, leaving Tái-oh at home.

"Now," said the Eagle, "untie this thong from my leg, friend, and get astride my neck, and we will go."

The string was soon untied, and Tái-oh got astride the neck of the great bird, which rose up into the air as though it carried no weight at all. It circled over the town a long time, and the people cried out with wonder and fear at seeing an Eagle with a boy on his back. Then they sailed out over the fields, where Tái-oh's parents and his sister were at work; and all the three began to cry, and went home in great sorrow.

The Eagle kept soaring up and up until they came to the very sky. There in the blue was a little door, through which the Eagle flew. Alighting on the floor of the sky, he let Tái-oh down from his back, and said:

"Now, you wait here, friend, while I go and see my people," and off he flew.

Tái-oh waited three days, and still the Eagle did not return; so he became uneasy and started out to see what he could find. After wandering a long way, he met an old Spider-woman.

"Where are you going, my son?" she asked.

"I am trying to find my friend, the Eagle."

"Very well, then, I will help you. Come into my house."

"But how can I come into so small a door?" objected Tái-oh.

"Just put your foot in, and it will open big enough for you to enter."

So Tái-oh put his foot in, and, sure enough, the door opened wide, and he went into the Spider's house and sat down.

"Now," said she, "you will have some trouble in getting to the house of your friend, the Eagle, for to get there you will have to climb a dreadful ladder. It is well that you came to me for help, for that ladder is set with sharp arrow-heads and knives of flint, so that if you tried to go up it, it would cut your legs off. But I will give you this sack of sacred herbs to help you. When you come to the ladder, you must chew some of the herbs and spit the juice on the ladder, which will at once become smooth for you."[1]

Tái-oh thanked the Spider-woman and started off with the sack. After awhile he came to the foot of a great ladder, which went away up out of sight. Its sides and rungs were bristling with keen arrow-heads, so that no living thing could climb it; but when Tái-oh chewed some of the magic herb and spat upon the ladder, all the sharp points fell off, and it was so smooth that he climbed it without a single scratch.

After a long, long climb, he came to the top of the ladder, and stepped upon the roof of the Eagles' house. But when he came to the door he found it so bristling with arrow-points that whoever might try to enter would be cut to pieces. Again he chewed some of the herb, and spat upon the door;

---

[1] This recalls a superstition of the Peruvian mountain Indians, ancient and modern. The latter I have often seen throwing upon a stone at the crest of a mountain pass the quid of coca-leaves they had been chewing. They believe such use of this sacred herb propitiates the spirits and keeps off the terrible *soroche*, or mountain-sickness; and that it also makes veins of metal easier to be worked — softening the stone, even as it did for Tái-oh.

and at once all the points fell off, and he entered safely, and inside he found his Eagle-friend, and all the Eagle-people. His friend had fallen in love with an Eagle-girl and married her, and that was the reason he had not returned sooner.

Tái-oh stayed there some time, being very nicely entertained, and enjoyed himself greatly in the strange sky-country. At last one of the wise old Eagle-men came to him and said:

"Now, my son, it is well that you go home, for your parents are very sad, thinking you are dead. After this, whenever you seen an Eagle caught and kept captive, you must let it go; for now you have been in our country, and know that when we come home we take off our feather-coats and are people like your own."

So Tái-oh went to his Eagle-friend and said he thought he must go home.

"Very well," said the Eagle; "get on my neck and shut your eyes, and we will go."

So he got on, and they went down out of the sky, and down and down until at last they came to Moqui. There the Eagle let Tái-oh down among the wondering people, and, bidding him an affectionate good-by, flew off to his young wife in the sky.

Tái-oh went to his home loaded down with dried meat and tanned buckskin, which the Eagle had given him; and there was great rejoicing, for all had given him up as dead. And this is why, to this very day, the Moquis will not keep an Eagle captive, though nearly all the other Pueblo towns have all the Eagle-prisoners they can get.

XIX

THE NORTH WIND AND THE SOUTH WIND

NEARLY every nation has its folk-lore concerning Jack Frost and his anti-type. The cold North Wind is always the enemy of man, and the warm South Wind always his friend. The Quères pueblos of Acoma and Laguna have an allegorical folk-story, in which the good spirit of heat defeats his icy-hearted rival.

Once, long ago, the *ta-pó-pe* (governor) of Acoma had a beautiful daughter, for whom many of the young men had asked in vain, for she would have none of them. One day there came climbing up the stone ladder to the cliff-built pueblo a tall and handsome stranger. His dress glistened with white crystals, and his face, though handsome, was very stern. The fair *kot-chin-á-ka* (chief's daughter), bending at a pool in the great rock to fill her water-jar, saw and admired him as he came striding proudly to the village; and he did not fail to notice the dusky beauty. Soon he asked for her in due form; and in a little while they were to be married.

But, with the coming of Shó-kee-ah — for that was the name of the handsome stranger — a sad change befell Acoma. The water froze in the springs and the corn withered in the fields. Every morning Shó-kee-ah left the town and went away to his home in the far North; and every evening he returned, and the air grew chill around. The people could raise no crops, for the bitter cold killed all that they planted, and nothing would grow but the thorny cactus. To keep from starving, they had to eat the cactus-leaves, roasting them first to remove the sharp thorns. One day, when the *kot-chin-á-ka* was roasting cactus-leaves, there came another handsome stranger with a sunny smile and stood beside her.

"What dost thou there?" he asked; and she told him.

"But do not so," said the young man, giving her an ear of green corn. "Eat this, and I will bring thee more."

So saying, he was gone; but very soon he returned with such a load of green corn as the strongest man could not lift, and carried it to her house.

"Roast this," he said, "and when the people come to thee, give them each two ears, for hereafter there shall always be much corn."

She roasted the corn and gave it to the people, who took it eagerly, for they were starving. But soon Shó-kee-ah returned, and the warm, bright day grew suddenly cold and cloudy. As he put his foot on the ladder to come down into the house (all Pueblo rooms used to be entered only from the roof, and thousands are so yet) great flakes of snow fell around him; but Mí-o-chin, the newcomer, made it very warm, and the snow melted.

"Now," said Shó-kee-ah, "we will see which is more powerful; and he that is shall have the *kot-chin-á-ka*." Mí-o-chin accepted the challengé, and it was agreed that the contest should begin on the morrow and last three days. Mí-o-chin went to consult an old Spider-woman as to the best way to conquer his powerful rival, and she gave him the necessary advice.

Next day the people all gathered to see the trial of strength between the two wizards. Shó-kee-ah "made medicine," and caused a driving sleet and a bitter wind that froze all waters. But Mí-o-chin built a fire and heated small stones in it, and with them caused a warm South Wind, which melted the ice. On the second day, Shó-kee-ah used more powerful incantations, and made a deep snow to cover the world; but again Mí-o-chin brought his South Wind and chased away the snow. On the third day Shó-kee-ah used his strongest spell, and it rained great icicles, until everything was buried under them. But when Mí-o-chin built his fire and heated the stones, again the warm South Wind drove away the ice and dried the earth. So it remained to Mí-o-chin; and the defeated Shó-kee-ah went away to his frozen home in the North, leaving Mí-o-chin to live happy ever after with the *kot-chin-á-ka*, whom he married amid the rejoicing of all the people of Acoma.

9

XX

THE TOWN OF THE SNAKE-GIRLS

IN the times that were farthest back, the forefathers of those who now dwell in Isleta were
scattered about in many small villages.   You have
already heard the myths of how the inhabitants of
several villages finally abandoned their homes and
came to live in the one big town of the Tée-wahn.
Three miles north of Isleta, amid the sandy plain
of Los Padillas, stands the strange round mesa of
Shee-em-tóo-ai.   It is a circular "island" of hard,
black lava, cut off from the long lava cliffs which
wall the valley of the Rio Grande on the west.   Its
level top, of over fifty acres, is some two hundred
feet above the plain; the last fifty feet being a
stern and almost unbroken cliff.   Upon its top are
still visible the crumbling ruins of the pueblo of
Poo-reh-tú-ai — a town deserted, as we are histori-
cally sure, over three hundred and fifty years ago.
The mound outlines of the round *estufa*, the houses
and the streets, are still easy to be traced, and bits
of pottery, broken arrow-heads, and other relics,
still abound there.   In history we know no more of
the pueblo than that it was once there, but had
been abandoned already when Coronado passed in

1540; but my aboriginal friends and fellow-citizens of Shee-eh-whíb-bahk have an interesting legend of the pueblo of Poo-reh-tú-ai and the cause which led to its abandonment.

When the mesa town was inhabited, so was Isleta; and, being but three miles apart, the inter-communication was constant. At one time, four hundred years ago or more, there lived in Isleta a very handsome youth whose name was K'oo-ah-máh-koo-hóo-oo-aí-deh—which means Young-Man-Who-Embraces-a-Corncob.

In spite of this serious burden of a title, the young man was greatly admired, and had many friends.   Probably they called him something else "for short," or people would n't have had time to associate with him.   There were two sisters, very pretty girls, living in Poo-reh-tú-ai, and they fell very seriously in love, both with this same youth. But he had never really found out how handsome he was, and so thought little about girls anyhow, caring more to run fastest in the races and to kill the most game in the hunts.   The sisters, finding that he would not notice their shy smiles, began to make it in their way to pass his house whenever they came to Isleta, and to say *hin-a-kú-pui-yoo* (good morning) as they met him on the road.   But he paid no attention to them whatever, except to be polite; and even when they sent him the modest little gift which means "there is a young lady who loves you!" he was as provokingly in-different as ever.

After long coquetting in vain, the girls began to hate him as hard as before they had loved him.

They decided, no doubt, that he was *oó-teh*, the Tée-wahn word for "a mean old thing"; and finally one proposed that they put him out of the way, for both sisters, young and pretty as they were, were witches.

"We will teach him," said one.

"Yes," said the other, "he ought to be punished; but how shall we do it?"

"Oh, we will invite him to play a game of *mahkhúr*, and then we'll fix him. I'll go now and make the hoop."

The witch-sisters made a very gay hoop, and then sent word to the youth to meet them at the sacred sand-hill, just west of Isleta, as they had important business with him. Wondering what it could be, he met them at the appointed time and place.

"Now, Brother Young-Man-Who-Embraces-a-Corncob," said the eldest sister, "we want to amuse ourselves a little, so let us have a game of *mahkhúr*. We have a very nice hoop to play it. You go half-way down the hill and see if you can catch it when we roll it to you. If you can, you may have the hoop; but if you fail, you come and roll it to us and we'll see if we can catch it."

So he went down the hill and waited, and the girls sent the bright wheel rolling toward him. He was very nimble, and caught it "on the fly"; but that very instant he was no longer the tall, handsome Young-Man-Who-Embraces-a-Corncob, but a poor little Coyote, with great tears rolling down his cheeks. The witch-sisters came laughing and taunting him, and said:

"You see it would have been better to marry us! But now you will always be a Coyote and an outcast from home. You may roam to the north and to the south and to the west, but never to the east" (and therefore not back to Isleta).

The Coyote started off, still weeping; and the two wicked sisters went home rejoicing at their success. The Coyote roamed away to the west, and at last turned south. After a time he came across a party of Isleteños[1] returning from a trading-trip to the Apache country. He sneaked about their camp, snapping up odd scraps—for he was nearly starved. In the morning the Indians spied this Coyote sitting and watching them at a little distance, and they set their dogs on him. But the Coyote did not run; and when the dogs came to him they merely sniffed and came away without hurting him—though every one knows that the dog and the Coyote have been enemies almost ever since the world began. The Indians were greatly astonished; and one of them, who was a medicine-man, began to suspect that there was something wrong. So, without saying anything to the others, he walked over to the Coyote and said: "Coyote, are you Coyote-true, or somebody bewitched?" But the Coyote made no reply. Again the medicine-man asked: "Coyote, are you a man?" At this the Coyote nodded his head affirmatively, while tears rolled from his eyes.

"Very well, then," said the medicine-man, "come with me." So the Coyote rose and followed him to the camp; and the medicine-man fed and cared

1 Pronounced Eez-lay-táyn-yos.

for him as the party journeyed toward Isleta. The
last night they camped at the big barranca, just
below the village; and here the medicine-man told
his companions the story of the bewitchment,—for
the Coyote had already told him,—and they were
all greatly astonished, and very sad to learn that
this poor Coyote was their handsome friend, K'oo-
ah-máh-koo-hóo-oo-aí-deh.

"Now," said the medicine-man, "we will make
a nice hoop and try a game." He made it, and
said to the Coyote: "Friend, go and stand over
there; and when I roll this hoop toward you, you
must jump and put your head through it before it
stops rolling or falls over upon its side."

The Coyote stood off, and the medicine-man
sent the hoop rolling toward him very hard. Just
as it came near enough the Coyote made a wonderful jump and put his head squarely through the
middle of it—and there, instead of the gaunt Coyote, stood the Young-Man-Who-Embraces-a-Corncob, handsome and well and strong as ever. They
all crowded around to congratulate him and to listen
to what had befallen him.

"Now," said the medicine-man, "when we get
home, the two witch-sisters will come to congratulate you, and will pretend not to know anything of
the trouble that befell you, and when you see them
you must invite *them* to a game of *mah-khúr.*"

It all came about as he said. When the party
got back to Isleta all the people welcomed the
young man whose mysterious disappearance had
made all sad. The news of his return spread rapidly, and soon reached the village of Poo-reh-tú-ai.

In a day or two the witch-sisters came to Isleta,
bringing on their heads baskets of the choicest
foods and other gifts, which they presented to him
in the most cordial manner.   To see how they
welcomed him, one would never fancy that they
had been the wicked causes of his suffering.   He
played his part equally well, and gave no sign
that he saw through their duplicity.   At last, when
they were about to start home, he said: " Sisters,
let us come to the sand-hill to-morrow to play a
little game."

An invitation—or rather a challenge—of that
sort must be accepted under all Indian etiquette;
and the witch-sisters agreed.   So at the appointed
hour they met him at the sacred hill.   He had
made a very beautiful hoop, and when they saw it
they were charmed, and took their positions at the
foot of the declivity. " One, two, three!" he counted;
and at the word " three!" sent the hoop rolling
down to them.   They both grabbed it at the same
instant, and lo! instead of the pretty, but evil-
minded sisters of Poo-reh-tú-ai, there lay two huge
rattlesnakes, with big tears falling from their eyes.
Young-Man-Who-Embraces-a-Corncob laid upon
their ugly, flat heads a pinch of the sacred meal,
and they ran out their tongues and licked it.

"Now," he said, "this is what happens to the
treacherous.   Here in these cliffs shall be your
home forever.   You must never go to the river, so
you will suffer with thirst and drag yourselves in
the dust all the days of your life."

The   Young-Man-Who-Embraces-a-Corncob
went back to Isleta, where he lived to a ripe old

age. As for the snakes, they went to live in the
cliffs of their own mesa. The people of Poo-reh-
tú-ai soon learned of the fate of the witch-sisters,
and knew that those two great snakes, with tears
in their eyes, were they. That was the beginning of
the downfall of Poo-reh-tú-ai; for the people grew
fearful of one another, lest there might be many
more witches, unbeknown, among them. The dis-
trust and discontent grew rapidly — for to this day
nothing on earth will disrupt any Indian community so quickly or so surely as the belief that some
of the people are witches. In a very short time
the people decided to abandon Poo-reh-tú-ai altogether. Most of them migrated to the Northwest,
and I have not as yet found even a legend to tell
what became of them. The rest settled in Isleta,
where their descendants dwell to this day. There
are old men here now who claim that their great-
grandfathers used to see the two huge rattlesnakes basking on the cliffs of the mesa of Shee-
em-tóo-ai, and that the snakes always wept when
people came near them.

XXI

THE DROWNING OF PECOS

TWENTY-FIVE miles southeast of Santa Fé, New Mexico, lie the deserted ruins of the ancient Pueblo town of Pecos. The village was finally abandoned by the Indians in 1840; and their neat houses of adobe bricks and stone, and their quaint adobe church, have sadly fallen to decay. The history of the abandonment of Pecos is by no means startling; but the Indian tradition — for they have already added this to their countless myths — is decidedly so. The story is related by two aged Pecos Indians who still live in the pueblo of Jemez.

"Now, this is a true story," said my informant, an Isleteño, who had often heard it from them.

Once Pecos was a large village, and had many people.[1] But it came that nearly all of them had the evil road, and in the whole town were but five True Believers (in the Indian religion). These were an old woman, her two sons, and two other young men. Agostin, her elder son, was a famous

---

[1] It was, indeed, the largest pueblo in New Mexico, having at one time a population of about 2000.

hunter, and very often went to the mountains with a friend of his who had an evil spirit — though Agostin was not aware of that.

One day the friend invited Agostin to go hunting, and next day they went to the mountains. Just at the foot they found a herd of deer, one of which Agostin wounded. The deer fled up the mountain, and the two friends followed by the drops of blood. Half-way to the top they came to a second herd, which ran off to the right of the trail they were following, and the evil-spirited friend went in pursuit of them, while Agostin kept on after the one he had wounded.

He came at last to the very top of the mountain, and there of a sudden the trail ceased. Agostin hunted all about, but in vain, and at last started down the other side of the mountain.

As he came to a deep cañon he heard singing, and, peering cautiously through the bushes, he saw a lot of witch-men sitting around a fallen pine and singing, while their chief was trying to raise the tree.

Agostin recognized them all, for they were of Pecos, and he was much grieved when he saw his friend among them. Then he knew that the deer had all been witches, and that they had led him off on a false trail.

Greatly alarmed, he crept back to a safe distance, and then hurried home and told his aged mother all that had happened, asking her if he should report it to the Cacique.

"No," said she, with a sigh, "it is of no use; for he, too, has the evil road. There are but few

True Believers left, and the bad ones are trying to use us up."

Among the five good people was one of the Cum-pah-whit-lah-wen (guards of the medicine-men); and to him Agostin told his story. But he also said: "It is of no use. We are too few to do anything."

At last the bad people falsely accused the old woman, saying that her power was more than that of all the medicine-men put together (which is a very serious charge, even to-day, among the Indians); and challenged her to come before all the people in the medicine-house and perform miracles with them, well knowing that she could not. The challenge was for life or death; whichever side won was to kill the others without being resisted.

The poor old woman told her sons, with tears, saying: "Already we are killed. We know nothing of these things, and we may make ready to die."

"Nay, Nana," said Agostin.[1] "Despair not yet, but prepare lunch for Pedro [1] and me, that we go to other villages for advice. Perhaps there the medicine-men will tell us something."

So the mother, still weeping, made some tortillas, and, strapping these to their belts, the young men set out.

Pedro, the younger, went east, and Agostin took the road to the north. Whatever person they met, or to whatever village they came, they were to seek advice.

When Agostin came to the foot of the mountains, he was very thirsty, but there was no water. As he

---

1 Pronounced Ah-gohs-téen and Páy-droh.

entered a gorge he saw Hyo-kwáh-kwah-báy-deh, a little bird which builds its nest with pebbles and clay in the crannies of the cliffs, and is of exactly the same color as the sandstones. He thought, "Ah, little bird, if you could speak I would ask you where there is water, for I am fainting with thirst, and dare not eat, for that would make it worse!"

But the little bird, knowing his thought, said:

"Friend Agostin, I see that you are one of the True Believers, and I will show you where there is water; or wait, I will go and bring you some, for it is very far." And off he flew.

Agostin waited, and presently the little bird came back, bringing an acorn-cup full of water. Then Agostin's heart sank, and he thought: "Alas! what good will that drop do me?"

But the little bird replied: "Do not think that way, friend. Here is enough, and even more; for when you drink all you wish, there will still be some left."

And so it was. Agostin drank and drank, then ate some tortillas and drank again; and when he was satisfied, the acorn-cup was still nearly full.

Then the little bird said: "Now come, and I will lead you. But when we come to the top of the mountain, and I say, 'We are at the top,' you must say, 'No, we are down in the mountain—at the bottom of it.' Do not forget."

Agostin promised, and the little bird flew in front of him. At last they were at the top, and the little bird said:

"Here we are, friend, at the top."

"No," answered Agostin, "we are down in the mountain—at the bottom of it."

Three times the little bird repeated his words, and three times Agostin made the same answer.

At the third reply they found themselves in a room in the mountain. There was a door in front of them, and beside it stood a Cum-pah-whit-lah-wíd-deh (guard), who said to Agostin—for the little bird had disappeared:

"Son, how came you here, where none ever think of coming? Do you think you are a man?"

Agostin told the whole story of the witches' challenge, and of how he had gone out to seek advice, and of how the little bird had brought him here, and the guard said:

"You are coming with the thought of a man; so now come in," and he opened the door.

But when Agostin entered the inner room, which was so large that no end could be seen, he found himself in the presence of the Trues in human shape.

There sat the divinities of the East, who are white; and of the North, who are blue; and beyond them were the sacred animals—the mountain lion, the eagle, bear, buffalo, badger, hawk, rabbit, rattlesnake, and all the others that are of the Trues. Agostin was very much afraid, but the guard said to him:

"Do not fear, son, but take the heart of a man, and pray to all sides." So he faced to the six sides, praying. When he had finished, one of the Trues spoke to him, and said:

"What can it be that brought you here? Take the heart of a man and tell us."

Then Agostin told his whole story; after which the Trues said to him:

"Do not be worried, son. We will help you out of that."

The principal True of the East said:

"Son, I will give you the clothes you must wear when you are in the medicine-house for the contest of power"; and he gave Agostin four dark-blue breech-clouts and some moccasins for himself and the three other good young men, and a black *manta* (robe) and pair of moccasins for his mother.

"Now," said the True, "the evil-spirited ones will have this medicine-making contest in the *es-tufa*,[1] and when you enter, you five, you must all be dressed in these clothes. The people will all be there, old and young, and there will hardly be room for you to stand; and they will all sneer at you and spit upon you. But do not be sorry. And take this cane to hold between you. Let your mother take it with one hand at the bottom, then the Whit-lah-wíd-deh's hand, then her other hand, and then his other hand; and last your brother's hand, your hand, then his other hand, and your other hand at the top of all. And when you say, 'We are at the top of the mountain,' he must answer, 'No, we are down in the mountain—at the bottom of it.' This you must keep saying. Now go, son, with the heart of a man."

Then the Whit-lah-wíd-deh led Agostin out, and the little bird showed him the way down the mountain.

When he reached home it was the afternoon of

1 Where it is sacrilegious to make medicine.

the appointed day, and in the evening the medicine-making contest for life or death was to come.

In a little while the younger brother arrived, with his new clothes and moccasins torn to shreds; for he had traveled far in a rough country, without meeting a soul from whom to ask advice.

Agostin called together the four other True Believers, and told them all that had happened and what they must do, giving them the sacred clothing.

In the evening they went to the *estufa*, which was crowded with the witch-people, so that they had barely room to stand.

Then the evil-spirited ones began to make medicine, and turned themselves into bears, coyotes, crows, owls, and other animals. When they were done, they said to the old woman:

"Now it is your turn. We will see what you can do."

"I know nothing about these things," she said, "but I will do what I can, and the Trues will help me."

Then she and the four young men took hold of the sacred cane as the Trues had showed Agostin.

"We are on the top of the mountain," said he.

"No," answered his brother, "we are down in the mountain—at the bottom of it."

This they said three times. At the third saying the people heard on all sides the *guajes* of the Trues.[1] At the same moment the ladder[2] was jerked violently up out of the room, so that no one could get out.

1 The thunder is said by the Tée-wahn to be the sacred dance-rattle of their gods.
2 The only entrance to any *estufa* is by a ladder let down through a door in the roof.

Then the two brothers repeated their words again, and at the third saying the thunder began to roar outside, and all could hear plainly the singing and the *guajes* of the Trues. It began to rain violently, and the water poured down through the roof-door, and the lightning stuck its tongue in. The brothers kept repeating their words, and soon the water was knee-deep. But where the five True Believers stood, holding the cane, the floor was dusty. Soon the flood came to the waists of the witch-people, and then to their necks, and the children were drowning. Then they cried out to the old woman:

"Truly, mother, your power is greater than ours. We submit."

But she paid no attention to them, and her sons continued their words, and the water kept pouring in until it touched the very ceiling. But all around the five it stood back like a wall, and they were on dry ground.

At last all the evil-spirited ones were drowned. Then the rain ceased and the water departed as fast as it had come. The ladder came down through the roof-door again, and the five True Believers climbed out and went to their homes.

But it was very desolate, for they were the only survivors. Their nearest relatives and dearest friends had perished with the other witch-people. At last they could no longer bear to live in the lonely valley, and they decided to live elsewhere. On the way the old mother and one of the men died. Agostin went to the pueblo of Cochití, and Pedro and the Whit-lah-wíd-deh settled in the pueblo of Jemez, where they are still living (or were in the spring of 1891).

Such is the Indian version of the abandonment of the great pueblo which Coronado—that wonderful Spanish explorer—found in 1540. As a matter of fact, the Hyó-qua-hoon, or people of Pecos, had dwindled away by war, epidemics, and the like, until only five were left; and in 1840 these lonely survivors moved to other pueblos, and abandoned their ruined town forever. But the story is very valuable, not only for the glimpse it affords of some of their most secret beliefs, but also as showing how folk-stories of the most aboriginal stamp are still coined.

Witchcraft is still a serious trouble in all the pueblos, despite the efforts of the medicine-men, whose special duty it is to keep down the witches. One little pueblo called Sandia is dying out—as many others have done before it—because the medicine-men are quietly killing those whom they suspect of being witches. In 1888 a very estimable Indian woman of that town was slain by them in the customary way,—shot through from side to side with an arrow,—and this form of execution is still practised.

In Isleta they fear the Americans too much to indulge in witch-killing, for Albuquerque is only a few miles away. But it is only a little while ago that a young Isletan who was accused spent three months in the neck-stocks in our aboriginal prison, and much of the time had to "ride the horse," sitting with his legs crossed upon the adobe floor and the heavy weight of the stocks pressing him down, a torture worthy of the Inquisition. The case was kept out of the American courts only by the payment of a large sum to his parents by his accusers.

One whose eyes or lids look red is always regarded with suspicion here, for witch-people are supposed not to sleep at night, but to change themselves into animals and roam over the world. Eccentric actions also lay one open to accusation; and when I first came here I was dangerously near being classed with the witches because, to amuse my dusky little neighbors, I imitated various animal cries to their great edification, but to the very serious doubt of their elders. The fact that they doubt whether Americans know enough to be first-class witches was largely instrumental in saving me from serious danger.

The Ants that Pushed on the Sky

XXII

A VERY ancient and characteristic story about the origin of Isleta is based on the historic fact that part of its founders came from east of the Manzano Mountains, from one of the prehistoric pueblos whose ruins are now barely visible in those broad plains.

Once upon a time there lived in one of those villages (so runs the story) a young Indian named Kahp-too-óo-yoo, the Corn-stalk Young Man. He was not only a famous hunter and a brave warrior against the raiding Comanches, but a great wizard ; and to him the Trues had given the power of the clouds. When Kahp-too-óo-yoo willed it, the glad rains fell, and made the dry fields laugh in green ;

and without him no one could bring water from the sky. His father was Old-Black-Cane, his mother was Corn-Woman, and his two sisters were Yellow-Corn-Maiden, and Blue-Corn-Maiden.

Kahp-too-óo-yoo had a friend, a young man of about the same age. But, as is often true, the friend was of a false heart, and was really a witch, though Kahp-too-óo-yoo never dreamed of such a thing.

The two young men used to go together to the mountains to get wood, and always carried their bows and arrows, to kill deer and antelopes, or whatever game they might find.

One day the false friend came to Kahp-too-óo-yoo, and said:

"Friend, let us go to-morrow for wood, and to hunt."

They agreed that so they would do. Next day they started before sunrise, and came presently to the spot where they gathered wood. Just there they started a herd of deer. Kahp-too-óo-yoo followed part of the herd, which fled to the north-west, and the friend pursued those that went south-west. After a long, hard chase, Kahp-too-óo-yoo killed a deer with his swift arrows, and brought it on his strong back to the place where they had separated. Presently came the friend, very hot and tired, and with empty hands; and seeing the deer, he was pinched with jealousy.

"Come, friend," said Kahp-too-óo-yoo. "It is well for brothers to share with brothers. Take of this deer and cook and eat; and carry a part to your house, as if you had killed it yourself."

THE ANTS THAT PUSHED ON THE SKY   149

"Thank you," answered the other coldly, as one who will not; but he did not accept.

When they had gathered each a load of wood, and lashed it with rawhide thongs in bundles upon their shoulders, they trudged home—Kahp-too-óo-yoo carrying the deer on top of his wood. His sisters received him with joy, praising him as a hunter; and the friend went away to his house, with a heavy face.

Several different days when they went to the mountain together, the very same thing came to pass. Kahp-too-óo-yoo killed each time a deer; and each time the friend came home with nothing, refusing all offers to share as brothers. And he grew more jealous and more sullen every day.

At last he came again to invite Kahp-too-óo-yoo to go; but this time it was with an evil purpose that he asked. Then again the same things happened. Again the unsuccessful friend refused to take a share of Kahp-too-óo-yoo's deer; and when he had sat long without a word, he said:

"Friend Kahp-too-óo-yoo, now I will prove you if you are truly my friend, for I do not think it."

"Surely," said Kahp-too-óo-yoo, "if there is any way to prove myself, I will do it gladly, for truly I am your friend."

"Then come, and we will play a game together, and with that I will prove you."

"It is well! But what game shall we play, for here we have nothing?"

Near them stood a broken pine-tree, with one great arm from its twisted body. And looking at it, the false friend said:

"I see nothing but to play the *gallo* race; and because we have no horses[1] we will ride this arm of the pine-tree—first I will ride, and then you."

So he climbed the pine-tree, and sat astride the limb as upon a horse, and rode, reaching over to the ground as if to pick up the chicken.[2]

"Now you," he said, coming down; and Kahp-too-óo-yoo climbed the tree and rode on the swinging branch. But the false friend bewitched the pine, and suddenly it grew in a moment to the very sky, carrying Kahp-too-óo-yoo.

"We do this to one another," taunted the false friend, as the tree shot up; and taking the wood, and the deer which Kahp-too-óo-yoo had killed, he went to the village. There the sisters met him, and asked:

"Where is our brother?"

"Truly I know not, for he went northwest and I southwest; and though I waited long at the meeting-place, he did not come. Probably he will soon return. But take of this deer which I killed, for sisters should share the labors of brothers."

But the girls would take no meat, and went home sorrowful.

Time went on, and still there was no Kahp-too-óo-yoo. His sisters and his old parents wept always, and all the village was sad. And soon the crops grew yellow in the fields, and the springs failed, and the animals walked like weary shadows; for Kahp-too-óo-yoo, he who had the power of the

[1] This mention of the horse is, of course, modern. I think it is an interpolation. The rest of the story bears traces of great antiquity.
[2] In imitation of one of the most popular and exciting sports of the Southwestern Indians and Mexicans.

clouds, was gone, and there was no rain. And then perished all that is green; the animals fell in the brown fields; and the gaunt people who sat to warm themselves in the sun began to die there where they sat. At last the poor old man said to his daughters:

"Little daughters, prepare food, for again we will go to look for your brother."

The girls made cakes of the blue corn-meal for the journey; and on the fourth day they started. Old-Black-Cane hobbled to the south, his wife to the east, the elder girl to the north, and the younger to the west.

For a great distance they traveled; and at last Blue-Corn-Maiden, who was in the north, heard a far, faint song. It was so little that she thought it must be imaginary; but she stopped to listen, and softly, softly it came again:

Tó-ai-fóo-ni-hlóo-hlim,
Eng-k'hai k'háhm ;
Eé-eh-bóori-kóon-hlee-oh,
Ing-k'hai k'háhm.
Ah-ee-ái, ah-hee-ái,
Aim !

(Old-Black-Cane
My father is called;
Corn-Woman
My mother is called.
Ah-ee-ái, ah-hee-ái,
Aim !)

When she heard this, Blue-Corn-Maiden ran until she came to her sister, and cried:

"Sister! Sister! I think I hear our brother somewhere in captivity.   Listen!"

Trembling, they listened; and again the song
came floating to them, so soft, so sad that they
wept—as to this day their people weep when a
white-haired old man, filled with the memories of
Kahp-too-óo-yoo, sings that plaintive melody.

"Surely it is our brother!" they cried; and off
they went running to find their parents.   And
when all listened together, again they heard the
song.

"Oh, my son!" cried the poor old woman, "in
what captivity do you find yourself?   True it is
that your father is Old-Black-Cane, and I, your
mother, am called Corn-Woman.   But why do you
sing thus?"

Then all four of them began to follow the song,
and at last they came to the foot of the sky-reach-
ing pine; but they could see nothing of Kahp-too-
óo-yoo, nor could their cries reach him.   There, on
the ground, were his bow and arrows, with strings
and feathers eaten away by time; and there was
his pack of wood, tied with the rawhide thong,
ready to be taken home.   But after they had
searched everywhere, they could not find Kahp-
too-óo-yoo; and finally they went home heavy at
heart.

At last it happened that P'ah-whá-yoo-óo-deh,
the Little Black Ant, took a journey and went up
the bewitched pine, even to its top in the sky.
When he found Kahp-too-óo-yoo there a prisoner,
the Little Black Ant was astonished, and said:

"Great *Kah-báy-deh* [Man of Power], how comes

SOUTH, EAST, NORTH, AND WEST IN SEARCH OF KAHP-TOO-ÓO-YOO.

it that you are up here in such a condition, while
your people at home are suffering and dying for
rain, and few are left to meet you if you return?
Are you here of your free will?"

"No," groaned Kahp-too-óo-yoo; "I am here
because of the jealousy of him who was as my
brother, with whom I shared my food and labor,
whose home was my home, and my home his.   He
is the cause, for he was jealous and bewitched me
hither.   And now I am dying of famine."

"If that is so," said the Little Black Ant, "I will
be the one to help you"; and he ran down to the
world as fast as he could.   When he got there he
sent out the crier to summon all his nation, and
also that of the *In-toon*, the Big Red Ants.   Soon
all the armies of the Little Black Ants and the Big
Red Ants met at the foot of the pine, and held a
council.   They smoked the *weer* and deliberated
what should be done.

"You Big Red Ants are stronger than we who
are small," said the War-Captain of the Little
Black Ants, "and for that you ought to take the
top of the tree to work."

"*Een-dah!*" (No) said the War-Captain of the
Big Red Ants.   "If you think we are the stronger,
give us the bottom, where we can work more, and
you go to the top."

So it was agreed, and the captains made their
armies ready.   But first the Little Black Ants got
the cup of an acorn, and mixed in it corn-meal and
water and honey, and carried it up the tree.   They
were so many that they covered its trunk all the
way to the sky.

When Kahp-too-óo-yoo saw, his heart was heavy, and he thought: "But what good will that very little do me, for I am dying of hunger and thirst?"

"Nay, friend," answered the Captain of the Little Black Ants, who knew his thought. "A person should not think so. This little is enough, and there will be some left."

And it was so; for when Kahp-too-óo-yoo had eaten all he could, the acorn-cup was still nearly full. Then the ants carried the cup to the ground and came back to him.

"Now, friend," said the Captain, "we will do our best. But now you must shut your eyes till I say '*Ahw!*'"

Kahp-too-óo-yoo shut his eyes, and the Captain sent signals down to those at the foot of the tree. And the Little Black Ants above put their feet against the sky and pushed with all their might on the top of the pine; and the Big Red Ants below caught the trunk and pulled as hard as they could; and the very first tug drove the great pine a quarter of its length into the earth.

"*A hw!*" shouted the Captain of the Little Black
Ants, and Kahp-too-óo-yoo opened his eyes; but
he could see nothing below.

"Shut your eyes again," said the Captain, giving the signal.   Again the Little Black Ants
pushed mightily against the sky, and the Big Red
Ants pulled mightily from below; and the pine was
driven another fourth of its length into the earth.

"*A hw!*" cried the Captain; and when Kahp-too-
óo-yoo opened his eyes he could just see the big,
brown world.

Again he closed his eyes.   There was another
great push and pull, and only a quarter of the pine
was left above the ground.   Now Kahp-too-óo-yoo
could see, far below, the parched fields strewn with
dead animals, and his own village full of dying
people.

Again the Little Black Ants pushed and the Big
Red Ants pulled, and this time the tree was driven
clear out of sight, and Kahp-too-óo-yoo was left
sitting on the ground.   He hastily made a bow and
arrows and soon killed a fat deer, which he brought
and divided among the Little Black Ants and the
Big Red Ants, thanking them for their kindness.

Then he made all his clothing to be new, for he
had been four years a prisoner in the bewitched
tree, and was all in rags.   Making for himself
a flute from the bark of a young tree, he played
upon it as he strode homeward and sang:

> *Kahp-too-óo-yoo tú-mah-quee,*
> *Nah-chóor kwé-shay-tin,*
> *Nah-shúr kwé-shay-tin;*
> *Kahp-too-óo-yoo tú-mah-quee!*

(Kahp-too-óo-yoo has come to life again,
Is back to his home coming,
Blowing the yellow and the blue;
Kahp-too-óo-yoo has come to life again!)

As he walked and sang, the forgotten clouds came over him, and the soft rain began to fall, and all was green and good. But only so far as his voice reached came the rain; and beyond all was still death and drought. When he came to the end of the wet, he played and sang again; and again the rain fell as far as his voice was heard. This time the Fool-Boy, who was wandering outside the dying village, saw the far storm and heard the singing. He ran to tell Kahp-too-óo-yoo's parents; but nobody would believe a Foolish, and they sent him away.

KAHP-TOO-ÓO-YOO
CALLING THE RAIN.

When the Fool-Boy went out again, the rain fell on him and gave him strength, and he came running a second time to tell. Then the sisters came out of the house and saw the rain and heard the song; and they cried for joy, and told their parents to rise and meet him. But the poor old people were dying of weakness, and could not rise; and the sisters went alone. When they met him they fell on their knees, weeping; but Kahp-too-óo-yoo lifted them up and blessed them, gave an ear of blue corn to Blue-Corn-Maiden, and to Yellow-Corn-Maiden an ear of yellow corn, and brought them home.

As he sang again, the rain fell in the village; and when it touched the pinched faces of the dead they sat up and opened their mouths to catch it. And the dying crawled out to drink, and were strong again; and the withered fields grew green and glad.

When they came to the house, Kahp-too-óo-yoo blessed his parents, and then said:

"Little sisters, give us to eat."

But they answered, "How? For you have been gone these four years, and there was none to give us rain. We planted, but nothing came, and to-day we ate the last grain."

"Nay, little sisters," he said. "A person should not think so. Look now in the store-rooms, if there be not something there."

"But we have looked and looked, and turned over everything to try to find one grain."

"Yet look once more," he said; and when they opened the door, lo! there was the store-room piled to the roof with corn, and another room was full of wheat. Then they cried for joy, and began to roast the blue ears, for they were dying of hunger.

At the sweet smell of the roasting corn came the starving neighbors, crowding at the door, and crying:

"O Kahp-too-óo-yoo! Give us to taste one grain of corn, and then we will go home and die."

But Kahp-too-óo-yoo handed to each an ear, and said:

"Fathers, brothers, go now to your own houses, for there you will find corn as much as here." And when they went, it was so. All began to roast corn and to eat; and the dead in the houses awoke and were strong again, and all the village sang and danced.

From that time there was plenty of rain, for he who had the power of the clouds was at home again. In the spring the people planted, and in the fall the crops were so great that all the town could not hold them; so that which was left they brought to Shee-eh-whíb-bak (Isleta), where we enjoy it to this day.

As for the false friend, he died of shame in his house, not daring to come out; and no one wept for him.

XXIII

THE MAN WHO WOULD N'T KEEP SUNDAY

AMONG the folk-stories of the Pueblos which show at once that they are not of such antiquity as the rest, is this. It is plain that the story is post-Spanish—that it has been invented within the last three hundred and fifty years. That seems to us a long time to go back in the history of America, but to the Pueblos it is a trifling dot on the long line of their antiquity.

The following tale is an amusing instance of the fashion in which some of the myth-makers have mixed things. It is an Indian fairy tale, but with a Christian moral—which was learned from the noble and effective Spanish missionaries who toiled here.

Once upon a time, in a pueblo south of Isleta,—one of its old colonies known as P'ah-que-tóo-ai, the Rainbow Town, but deserted long ago,—there were two Indians who were great friends. They started in life with equal prospects, married young, and settled in the same town. But though friends, their natures were very different. One was a good man in his heart, and the other was bad. The good man always observed Sunday, but the other worked every day. The good man had better luck than the bad; and the latter became jealous. At last he said: "Friend, tell me, why is it that you always make more success than I?"

"Perhaps," answered Good, "because I keep Sunday, but work hard all the other days of the week, while you work every day."

Time went on, and both the friends accumulated considerable wealth in servants, stock, and ornaments. The good man let his servants rest on Sunday, but the bad made his work every day, and did not even give them time to smoke. Good prospered most, and had more servants, more stock, and more ornaments than Bad, who grew more jealous daily. At last Bad said to Good: "Friend, you say that you have good luck because you keep Sunday, but I 'll bet I am right in *not* keeping it."

"No," replied Good; "I 'll bet *I* am right, and that Sunday ought to be kept."

"Then I will bet all my stock against all your stock, and all my lands against your lands, and everything we have except our wives. To-morrow, be ready about breakfast-time, and we will go out into the public road and ask the first three men we meet which of us is right. And whichever gets the voice of the majority, he shall be the winner, and shall take all that is of the other."

Good agreed,—for an Indian cannot back out of a challenge,—and so the next morning the two friends took the public road. In a little while they met a man, and said to him: "Friend, we want your voice. Which of us is right, the one who observes Sunday and lets his *peons* rest then, or he who does not?"

Now it happened that this person was not a man, but an old devil who was taking a walk in human form; and he promptly answered: "Without doubt he is right who does not keep Sunday," and went his road.

"Aha!" said Bad to Good. "You see I got the first voice."

They started on again and soon met another man, to whom they asked the same. But it was the same old devil, and he gave them the same answer.

"Aha!" said Bad. "Now I have the second voice, you see."

Presently they met a third man, and asked him the same, and he answered the same; for it was the same old devil in another body.

"Aha!" said Bad, "I am the winner! Get down from that burro, and let me have her and her colt, for now all that was yours is mine, as we agreed."

Good got down from the burro with tears in his eyes, for he was thinking of his wife, and said:

"Now, friend, having gained all, you are going back to our home; but I shall not. Tell my wife that I am going to the next pueblo to seek work, and that I will not be back until I have earned as much as I have lost in this bet, or more; but tell her not to be sad."

Then they shook hands and parted, Bad riding home full of joy, and Good trudging off through the sand toward Isleta, which was the largest and wealthiest pueblo of the tribe. On the road night overtook him, and seeing an abandoned house in a field, he hastened to it for shelter from the cold of night. A portion of the roof still remained, with the *fogon* (corner fireplace) and chimney, and he began to brush a place to lie down. Now it happened that this house was the place where all the devils of that country used to meet at night; and before Good went to sleep he heard noises of the devils coming. He was very much frightened, and to hide himself climbed up into the chimney and stood upon its crosspiece.

In a moment the devils began to arrive singly or in pairs; and at last came the old devil — the very one who had played the trick on Good. He called the meeting to order, and asked them what they had been doing. A young devil arose and said:

"The next pueblo is the largest and wealthiest of this nation. For three weeks now, all its people, and all the people along that river, have been working at the spring from which the river comes, but have not been able to undo me. Three weeks ago I came to that spring and thought how nice it would be to stop up the spring, and how the people would swear if their gods did not send rain. So I stuck a big stone in the spring and stopped all the water; and ever since, the water will not come out, and the people work in vain, and they are dying of thirst, and all their stock. Now they will either forsake their gods and serve us, or die like the animals, thinking nothing of their past or future."

"Good!" said the old devil, rubbing his hands. "You have done well! But tell me — is there no way to open the spring?"

"There is only one way," said the young devil, "and one man could do that — but they will never think of it. If a man took a long stick, shaped like a sword, and went and stood on top of the stone, and struck it with the full length of the stick first east and west, and then north and south, the water would come out so hard that the stone would be thrown out upon the banks and the spring could never be stopped again."

"Is *that* the only way?" said the old devil. "You have done very well, for they certainly will never think to do that. Now for the next."

Then another young devil arose and reported this:

"I, too, have done something. In the pueblo across the mountain I have the daughter of the wealthiest man sick in bed, and she will never get well. All the medicine-men have tried in vain to cure her. She, too, will be ours."

"Good!" said the old devil. "But is there no way in which any one may cure her?"

"Yes, there is one way, but they never will think of that. If a person should carry her to the door just as the sun is rising, and hold her so that its very first rays would touch the top of her head, she would be well at once, and never could be made sick again."

"You are right," said the old devil, "they will never think of that. You have done well."

Just then a rooster crowed, and the old devil cried, "You have a road!" — which means, "an adjournment is in order." All the devils hurried away; and when they were gone, poor Good crawled down from the chimney half dead with fright, and hurried on toward Isleta. When he

got there he found the people in great trouble, for
their crops were withering and their cattle dying
for want of water.

"I see," thought Good to himself, "that these
devils told the truth about one thing, and so
perhaps they did about all. I will try to undo
them, even if I fail." Going to the Cacique he
asked what they would give him if he would open
the spring. The Cacique told the *principales*, and
they held a *junta*, and decided to let the stranger
name his own price.

"Well," said he, "I will do this if you will give
me half the value of the whole village."

They agreed, and asked how many men he
would need to help him, and when he would begin.

"I need no men. Lend me only a hard stick
the length of my outstretched arms, and a horse."

These were given him, and he went to the spring
alone. Leaping upon the stone he struck it with
the full length of the stick east and west, and then
north and south, and sprang nimbly to the bank.
At that very instant the water rushed out harder
than it had ever done. All the people and cattle
along the river came to the banks and drank and
revived. They began to irrigate their fields again,
and the dying crops grew green.[1] When Good got
back to the pueblo, half of all the grain and money

---

[1] Here, as in several other stories in this volume, is a touch of the arid
character of the Southwest. The country is always so dry that irrigation is
necessary in farming, and in very bad years the streams have not water even
for that. The Rio Grande itself frequently disappears in September between
certain points in its course in sandy New Mexico; and within ten miles below
Isleta I have seen its bed bone-dry. Ignorance of this fact has caused serious
blunders on the part of historians unfamiliar with the country of which they
wrote.

and dresses and ornaments were piled up in a
huge pile waiting for him, and half the horses and
cattle and sheep were waiting in big herds. It
was so that he had to hire a great many men to
help him home with his wealth, which was more
than any one person ever had before. He appointed a mayordomo to take charge of this cara-
van, and to meet him at a certain point on the way
home. He himself, taking a horse, rode away at
once to the other pueblo, where the rich man's
daughter was sick. Arriving at nightfall, he
stopped at the house of an old woman. While he
ate, she told him how sad was all the village; for
the girl who had been so kind to all was dying.

"But," said he, "I can cure her."

"*In-dah*," said the crone; "for all the medicine-
men have tried vainly, and how shall you?"

"But I can," he insisted; and at last the old
woman went to the rich man, and said there was a
stranger at her house who was sure he could cure
the girl.

The *rico* said: "Go and tell him to come here
quickly," and the old woman did so. When Good
came, the rich man said: "Are you he who says
he can cure my daughter?"

"I am the one."

"For how much will you cure her?"

"What will you give?"

"Half of all I have, which is much."

"It is well. To-morrow be ready, for I will
come just before the sun."

In the blue of the morning Good came and
waked the girl, and carried her to the door. In a

moment came the sun, and its first ray fell upon
her bent head.   In an instant she was perfectly
well, and stronger and prettier than ever.

That very day her father gladly divided all his
wealth into two equal shares, and gave half to
Good, who again had to hire many cow-boys and
men with *carretas* to help him transport all this.
At the appointed spot he found his mayordomo;
and putting all the stock together, with many
herders, and all the wagons full of corn and dresses
and ornaments and money together, started homeward, sending ahead a messenger on a beautiful
horse to apprise his wife.

When the jealous Bad saw this fine horse going
to the house of his friend, he ran over to see what
it meant; and while he was still there, Good arrived with all his wealth.   Filled with envy, Bad
asked him where he had got all this; and Good
told the whole story.

"Well," said Bad, "I will go there too, and perhaps I will hear something."   So off he rode on the
burro he had won from Good, till he came to the
deserted house, and climbed up in the chimney.

Soon the devils met, and the two young ones
told their chief that the spring had been opened
and the girl cured, and that neither could ever be
bewitched again.

"Somebody must have listened to us last night,"
said the old devil, greatly troubled.   "Search the
house."   In a little while they found the jealous
friend in the chimney, and supposing him to be the
one who had undone them, without mercy puffed
him to the place where devils live.

XXIV

THE BRAVE BOBTAILS

WHEN it came old Anastacio's turn, one night, to tell a story to the waiting circle, it was several minutes before he responded to the quaint summons; and at last Lorenso repeated: "There is a tail to you, *compadre* Anastacio!" The words seemed to remind him of something; for he turned to his fat grandson, and said:

"Juan! Knowest thou why the Bear and the Badger have short tails? For once they had them long as Kéem-ee-deh, the Mountain Lion. *In-dah?* Then I will tell thee."

Once in the Days of the Old, it was that a young man lived here in Shee-eh-whíb-bak whom they called T'hoor-hlóh-ah, the Arrow of the Sun. He was not of the Tée-wahn, but a Ute, who was taken in war while yet a child. When the warriors brought him here, a Grandmother who was very poor took him for her son, and reared him, loving him greatly, and teaching him all the works of men. Coming to be a young man, he was a mighty hunter; but so good in his heart that he loved the animals as brothers, and they all loved

him.   When he went out to hunt, the first game he
killed he always dressed and left there for his an-
imal-friends to eat.   Sometimes it was Kéem-ee-
deh, king of the four-feet, who came to the feast
Sun-Arrow had made; and sometimes Kahr-naí-
deh, the Badger, who is best of all to dig, and who
showed Those of Old how to make their caves;
and sometimes the smaller ones.   They were all
grateful; for no other was so kind to feed them.

Now the Grandmother would never let Sun-
Arrow go to war, fearing that he would be killed;
and all the other young men laughed at him, because he had never taken the sacred *oak-bark*.
And when the others danced the great round-
dance, he had to stand alone.   So he was ashamed,
and vowed that he would prove himself a man;
and taking secretly his bow and arrows and his
thunder-knife, he went away by night alone, and
crossed the Eagle-Feather Mountains.

Now in that time there was always great war
with the Comanches, who lived in the plains.
They came often across the mountains and attacked Isleta by night, killing many people.   Their
chief was P'ee-kú-ee-fa-yíd-deh, or Red Scalp, the
strongest and largest and bravest of men.   For
many years all the warriors of Isleta had tried to
kill him, for he was the head of the war; but he
slew all who came against him.   He was very
brave, and painted his scalp red with *páh-ree*, so
that he might be known from far; and left his
scalp-lock very long, and braided it neatly, so that
an enemy might grasp it well.

Now Sun-Arrow met this great warrior; and

with the help of an old Spider-woman,[1] slew him and took his scalp. When the people of Isleta saw Sun-Arrow returning, the young men began to laugh and say: " Va! T'hoor-hlóh-ah has gone to make war again on the rabbits!'

But when he came into the plaza, saying nothing, and they saw that *oak-bark* which all knew, all cried out: " Come and look! For here is Sun-Arrow, who was laughed at — and now he has brought the bark of Red Scalp, whom our bravest have tried in vain to kill."

So when he had taken the scalp to the Cacique, and they had had the round-dance, and the days of purification were over, they called Sun-Arrow the greatest warrior of the Tée-wahn, and made him second to the Cacique. Then all who had daughters looked at him with good eyes, and all the maidens wished for so brave a husband. But he saw none of them, except the youngest daughter of the Cacique; for he loved her. When the Grandmother had spoken to the Cacique, and it was well, they brought the young people together, and gave them to eat of the betrothal corn — to Sun-Arrow an ear of the blue corn, and to her an ear of the white corn, because the hearts of maidens are whiter than those of men. When both had eaten the raw corn, every seed of it, the old folks said: " It is well! For truly they love each other. And now let them run the marrying-race."

Then all the people gathered yonder where are the ashes of the evil-hearted ones who were burned when Antelope Boy won for his people. And the

---

[1] About equivalent to our " fairy godmother."

elders marked a course, as of three miles, from there to the sacred sand-hill beside the Kú-mai. When they said the word, Sun-Arrow and the girl went running like young antelope, side by side. Up to the Place of the Bell they ran, and turned back running; and when they came to the people, the girl was a little in front, and all cried:

"It is well! For now Eé-eh-chah has won a husband, and she shall always be honored in her own house."

So they were married, and the Cacique blessed them. They made a house by the plaza,[1] and Sun-Arrow was given of the fields, that he might plant.

But of the maidens there was one who did not forgive Sun-Arrow that he would not look at her; and in her heart she thought to pay him. So she went to a Spider-woman,[2] and said: "Grandmother, help me! For this young man despised me, and now I will punish him."

Then the Spider-woman made an accursed prayer-stick of the feathers of the woodpecker, and spoke to the Ghosts, and said to the girl:

"It is well, daughter! For I am the one that will help you. Take only this Toad, and bury it in your floor, *this* way, and then ask T'hoor-hlóh-ah to come to your house."

The girl made a hole in her floor, and buried P'ah-foo-ée-deh, the Toad. Then she went to Sun-Arrow and said: "Friend T'hoor-hlóh-ah, come to my house a little; for I have to talk to you."

But when Sun-Arrow sat down in her house, his

1 Public square in the center of the pueblo.
2 Here equivalent to a witch.

feet were upon the floor over the hole; and in a moment the Toad grew very great, and began to swallow him by the feet. Sun-Arrow kicked and fought, for he was very strong. But he could do nothing; and in a little, he was swallowed to the knees. Then he called in a great voice for his wife; and all the people of the Tée-wahn came running with her. When they saw him so, they were very sad; and Eé-eh-chah took his hand, and the Grandmother took his other, and all the people helped them. But all were not so strong as the great Toad; and fast it was swallowing him, until he was at the waist. Then he said:

"Go, my people! Go, my wife! For it is in vain. Go from this place, that you may not see me. And pray to the Trues if they will help me." So they all went, mourning greatly.

In that time it came that Shee-íd-deh, the House-Mouse, stirred from his hole; and seeing Sun-Arrow *so*, he came to him, weeping.

"Oh, Friend Sun-Arrow!" he cried. "You who have been a father to us all, you who have fed us, and have proved yourself so brave—it is not deserved that you should be thus. But we for whom you have cared, we will be the ones to help you!"

Then Shee-íd-deh ran from the house until he found the Dog, and to him told it all. And Queeah-níd-deh, whose voice was big, ran out into the plains, up and down, *pregonando*[1] to all the animals; and they came hurrying from all places. Soon all the birds and all the four-feet were met in

[1] The technical (Spanish) word for the official heralding by which all announcements are still made among the Pueblos.

council in the room where Sun-Arrow was; and
the Mountain Lion was captain.   When he had
listened to them, he said:

"Now let each tribe of you choose from it one
who is young and strong, to give help to him who
has fed us.   For we cannot leave him to die so."

When every kind that walks or flies had chosen
its strongest one, the chosen stood out; and Kéem-
ee-deh called them by name to take their turns.

"Kóo-ah-raí-deh!" he called; and the Bluebird
of the mountains came to Sun-Arrow, who was
now swallowed up to his armpits.   Sun-Arrow
grasped her long tail with both hands, and she
flew and flew with all her might, not caring for the
pain, until her tail was pulled off.   But Sun-Arrow
was not budged a hair.

Then the captain called Ku-íd-deh, the Bear, to
try.   He gave his long tail to Sun-Arrow to hold;
and when he had counted "One, two, *three!*" he
pulled with a great pull, so hard that his whole tail
came off.   And still Sun-Arrow was not stirred.

Then it was to the Coyote.   But *he* said: "My
ears are stronger"; for he was a coward, and
would not give to pull on his pretty tail, of which
he is proud.   So he gave to Sun-Arrow to hold
by his ears, and began to pull backward.   But
soon it hurt him, and he stopped when his ears
were pulled forward.

"Now it is to you, Kahr-naí-deh," said the
Mountain Lion; and the Badger came out to try.
First he dug around Sun-Arrow, and gave him to
hold his tail.   Then he counted *three*, and pulled
greatly, so that his tail came off — and Sun-Arrow

was moved a very little.   But the Badger did not
fear the pain, and said:

" Let it be to me twice again, Kah-báy-deh."[1]

"It is well!" said the Mountain Lion.   " So let
it be."

So the Badger dug again, and gave the stump
of his tail, and pulled.   And Sun-Arrow was
loosened a little more; but the stump slipped
through his hands, for it was very short.

"*Around* me, friend," said the Badger, when
he had dug a third time; and Sun-Arrow clasped
his hands around the Badger's body, behind the
fore legs.   Then for the third time Kahr-naj́-deh
pulled — so mightily that he dragged Sun-Arrow
clear out from the Toad's mouth.   At that, all the
animals fell upon the wicked Toad, and killed it;
and gave thanks to Those Above for the deliver-
ance of their friend.

When they had prayed, Sun-Arrow thanked all
the animals, one by one; and to the Bluebird, the
Bear, and the Badger, he said:

" Friends, how shall I thank you who have suffered so much for me? And how can I pay you for
your help, and for the tails that you have lost?"
But to the Coyote he did not say a word.

Then said the Badger:

" Friend T'hoor-hlóh-ah, as for me, your hand
has always been held out to me.   You have fed
me, and have been as a father: I want no pay for
this tail that I have lost."

And the Bear and the Bluebird both answered
the same thing.

1 Commander.

So Sun-Arrow again gave them many thanks, and they went away to their homes. As for Sun-Arrow, he hurried to the Medicine House, where all the Tée-wahn were making medicine[1] that he might be saved. And when they saw him entering, his wife ran and cried on his shoulder, and all the people gave thanks to the Trues.

Sun-Arrow told them all that was; and when the Father-of-all-Medicine looked in the sacred *cajete*[2] he saw the evil-hearted girl paying the Spider-woman. Then the Cum-pah-whít-la-wen[3] went running with their bows and arrows, and brought the girl; and she was punished as are they that have the evil road. As for the Spider-woman, she was already dead of shame; for she knew all that had been.

In a time it came that his father-in-law the Cacique died; and they made Sun-Arrow Cacique in his place. For many years he was so, bringing great good to his people; for he was very wise.

As for the Bear, the Badger, and the Bluebird, they would never go to the medicine-men of their tribes to have their tails mended to grow again; for they were proud that they had suffered to help their friend. And to this very day they go with short tails, and are honored by all the animals, and by all True Believers. But Too-wháy-deh, the

---

1 Not compounding remedies, but going through the magic dance and incantations to which the Indians always resort in time of trouble. For a description of a medicine-making, see "Some Strange Corners of Our Country."
2 A jar of magic water, in which the chief conjuror is supposed to see all that is going on in the world.
3 Armed guards of the Medicine House.

coward, he who would not hurt himself with pulling
— he is a laughed-at to this day.   For his ears
cannot lie back, as is well for beasts, but always
point straight forward, as Sun-Arrow pulled them.

Any one who has ever seen the Coyote, or any
other of the wolf or fox tribe, must have noticed
the alert forward pricking of the ears.   Among the
Pueblos, any such peculiarity of nature—and particularly of animal life—is very sure to have a folk-
story hung to it.   It has always seemed to me that
the boy who always wants to know "why?" has a
better time of it among my Indian friends than anywhere else.   For there is always sure to be a why,
and an interesting one—which is much more satisfactory than only learning that "it's bedtime now,"
or that "I'm busy."

THE REVENGE of the FAWNS

XXV

"DON CARLOS," said Vitorino, throwing another log upon the fire, which caught his tall shadow and twisted it and set it dancing against the rocky walls of the cañon in which we were camped for the night, "did you ever hear why the Wolf and the Deer are enemies?" And as he spoke he stretched out near me, looking up into my face to see if I were going to be interested.

A few years ago it would have frightened me very seriously to find myself thus—alone in one of the remotest corners of New Mexico save for that swarthy face peering up into mine by the weird light of the camp-fire. A stern, quiet but manly face it seems to me now; but once I would have thought it a very savage one, with its frame of long, jet hair, its piercing eyes, and the broad streak of red paint across its cheeks. By this time, however, having lived long among the kindly Pueblos, I had shaken off that strange, ignorant prejudice against all that is unknown — which seems to be inborn in all of us — and wondered that I could ever have believed in that brutal maxim, worthy only of worse than savages, that "A good Indian is a dead Indian." For Indians are men, after all, and astonishingly like the rest of us when one really comes to know them.

I pricked up my ears — very glad at his hint of another of these folk-stories.

"No," I answered. "I have noticed that the Wolf and the Deer are not on good terms, but never knew the reason."

"*Sí, señor*," said he, — for Vitorino knows no English, and most of our talk was in Spanish, which is easier to me than the Tée-wahn language, — "that was very long ago, and now all is changed. But once the Wolf and the Deer were like brothers; and it is only because the Wolf did very wickedly that they are enemies. *Con su licencia, señor.*" [1]

"*Bueno; anda!*" [2]

So Vitorino leaned his shoulders against a convenient rock and began.

Once upon a time, when the Wolf and the Deer were friends, there were two neighbors in the country beyond the Rio Puerco, not far from where the

---

[1] "With your permission, sir."
[2] "All right; go ahead!"

pueblo of Laguna (a Quères town) now is. One
was a Deer-mother who had two fawns, and the
other a Wolf-mother with two cubs. They had
very good houses of adobe, just such as we live in
now, and lived like real people in every way. The
two were great friends, and neither thought of
going to the mountain for firewood or to dig
amole[1] without calling for the other to accompany
her.

One day the Wolf came to the house of the Deer
and said:

"Friend Peé-hlee-oh [Deer-woman], let us
go to-day for wood and *amole*, for I must wash
to-morrow."

"It is well, friend Káhr-hlee-oh," replied the
Deer.   "I have nothing to do, and there is food
in the house for the children while I am gone.
Toó-kwai! [Let us go]."

So they went together across the plain and into
the hills till they came to their customary spot.
They gathered wood and tied it in bundles to bring
home on their backs, and dug *amole*, which they
put in their shawls to carry.   Then the Wolf sat
down under a cedar-tree and said:

"*Ai!* But I am tired!   Sit down, friend Deer-
woman, and lay your head in my lap, that we may
rest."

"No, I am not tired," replied the Deer.

"But just to rest a little," urged the Wolf.   The
Deer good-naturedly lay down with her head in the
lap of her friend.   But soon the Wolf bent down
and caught the trusting Deer by the throat, and

[1] The root of the palmilla, generally used for soap throughout the Southwest.

killed her. That was the first time in the world
that any one betrayed a friend, and from that deed
comes all the treachery that is.

The false Wolf took off the hide of the Deer, and
cut off some of the meat and carried it home on her
load of *amole* and wood. She stopped at the house
of the Deer, and gave the Fawns some of the accursed meat, saying:

"Friends, Deer-babies, do not fear, but eat;
your mother met relatives and went to their house,
and she will not come to-night."

The Fawns were very hungry, and as soon as
the Wolf had gone home they built a big fire in the
fireplace and set the meat to cook. But at once it
began to sputter and to hiss, and the Fawn who
was tending it heard it cry, "Look out! look out!
for this is your mother!"

He was greatly frightened, and called his brother
to listen, and again the same words came from the
meat.

"The wicked old Wolf has killed our *nana!*
[mama]," they cried, and, pulling the meat from
the fire, they laid it gently away and sobbed themselves to sleep.

Next morning the Wolf went away to the
mountain to bring the rest of the deer-meat; and
when she was gone her Cubs came over to play
with the Fawns, as they were used to doing.
When they had played awhile, the Cubs said:

"*Pee-oo-wée-deh* [little Deer], why are you so
prettily spotted, and why do you have your eye-
lids red, while we are so ugly?"

"Oh," said the Fawns, "that is because when

we were little, like you, our mother put us in a room and smoked us, and made us spotted."

"Oh, Fawn-friends, can't you spot us, too, so that we may be pretty?"

So the Fawns, anxious to avenge the death of their mother, built a big fire of corn-cobs in the fireplace, and threw coyote-grass on it to make a great smoke. Then, shutting the Cubs into the room, they plastered up the door and windows with mud, and laid a flat rock on top of the chimney and sealed it around with mud; and climbing down from the roof, they took each other's hands and ran away to the south as fast as ever they could.

After they had gone a long way, they came to a Coyote. He was walking back and forth with one paw to his face, howling dreadfully with the tooth-ache. The Fawns said to him very politely:

"*Ah-bóo!* [poor thing]. Old-man friend, we are sorry your tooth hurts. But an old Wolf is chasing us, and we cannot stay. If she comes this way, asking about us, do not tell her, will you?"

"*Een-dah.* Little-Deer-friends, I will not tell her"—and he began to howl again with pain, while the Fawns ran on.

When the Wolf came to her home with the rest of the meat, the Cubs were not there; and she went over to the house of the Deer. It was all sealed and still; and when she pushed in the door, there were her Cubs dead in the smoke! When she saw that, the old Wolf was wild with rage, and vowed to follow the Fawns and eat them without mercy. She soon found their tracks leading away

THE WOLF, AND THE COYOTE WITH THE TOOTHACHE.

to the south, and began to run very swiftly in
pursuit.

In a little while she came to the Coyote, who
was still walking up and down, howling so that
one could hear him a mile away.   But not pitying
his pain, she snarled at him roughly:

"Say, old man! have you seen two Fawns running away?"

The Coyote paid no attention to her, but kept
walking with his hand to his mouth, groaning,
"*Mm-m-páh! Mm-m-páh!*"

Again she asked him the same question, more
snappishly, but he only howled and groaned.
Then she was very angry, and showed her big
teeth as she said:

"I don't care about your '*Mm-m-páh! Mm-m-
páh!*' Tell me if you saw those Fawns, or I'll eat
you this very now!"

"Fawns? *Fawns?*" groaned the Coyote — "I
have been wandering with the toothache ever since
the world began.   And do you think I have had
nothing to do but to watch for Fawns?   Go along,
and don't bother me."

So the Wolf, who was growing angrier all the
time, went hunting around till she found the trail,
and set to running on it as fast as she could go.

By this time the Fawns had come to where two
Indian boys were playing *k'wah-t'hím* [1] with their
bows and arrows, and said to them:

"Friends boys, if an old Wolf comes along and
asks if you have seen us, don't tell her, will you?"

The boys promised that they would not, and the

---

[1] A sort of walking archery.

Fawns hurried on. But the Wolf could run much faster, and soon she came to the boys, to whom she cried gruffly:

"You boys! did you see two Fawns running this way?"

But the boys paid no attention to her, and went on playing their game and disputing: "My arrow's nearest!" "No; mine is!" "'T ain't! Mine is!" She repeated her question again and again, but got no answer till she cried in a rage:

"You little rascals! Answer me about those Fawns, or I'll eat you!"

At that the boys turned around and said:

"We have been here all day, playing *k'wah-t'hím*, and not hunting Fawns. Go on, and do not disturb us."

So the Wolf lost much time with her questions and with finding the trail again; but then she began to run harder than ever.

In the mean time the Fawns had come to the bank of the Rio Grande, and there was *P'ah-chah-hlóo-hli*, the Beaver, hard at work cutting down a tree with his big teeth. And they said to him very politely:

"Friend Old-Crosser-of-the-Water, will you please pass us over the river?"

The Beaver took them on his back and carried them safely across to the other bank. When they had thanked him, they asked him not to tell the old Wolf about them. He promised he would not, and swam back to his work. The Fawns ran and ran, across the plain, till they came to a big black hill of lava that stands alone in the valley southeast of Tomé.

THE WOLF MEETS THE BOYS PLAYING WITH THEIR BOWS AND ARROWS.

"Here!" said one of the Fawns, "I am sure this must be the place our mother told us about, where the Trues of our people live. Let us look."

And when they came to the top of the hill, they found a trap-door in the solid rock. When they knocked, the door was opened and a voice called, "Enter!" They went down the ladder into a great room underground; and there they found all the Trues of the Deer-people, who welcomed them and gave them food.

When they had told their story, the Trues said:
"Fear not, friends, for we will take care of you."

And the War-captain picked out fifty strong young bucks for a guard.

By this time the Wolf had come to the river, and there she found the Beaver hard at work and grunting as he cut the tree.

"Old man!" she snarled, "did you see two Fawns here?"

But the Beaver did not notice her, and kept on walking around the tree, cutting it and grunting, "*Ah-oó-mah! Ah-oó-mah!*"

She was in a terrible rage now, and roared:
"I am not talking '*Ah-oó-mah!*' to you. I 'm asking if you saw two Fawns."

"Well," said the Beaver, "I have been cutting trees here by the river ever since I was born, and I have no time to think about Fawns."

The Wolf, crazy with rage, ran up and down the bank, and at last came back and said:

"Old man, if you will carry me over the river I will pay you; but if you don't, I 'll eat you up."

"Well, wait then till I cut around the tree three

times more," said the Beaver; and he made her
wait.   Then he jumped down in the water and
took her on his neck, and began to swim across.
But as soon as he came where the water was deep,
he dived to the bottom and stayed there as long as
he could.

"Ah-h-h!" sputtered the Wolf when he came to
the surface.   As soon as the Beaver got a breath,
down he went again; and so he kept doing all the
way across, until the Wolf was nearly drowned —
but she clung to his neck desperately, and he could
not shake her off.

When they came to the shore the old Wolf was
choking, coughing, and crying, and so mad that
she would not pay the Beaver as she had promised
— and from that day to this the Beaver will never
again ferry a Wolf across the river.

Presently she found the trail, and came running
to the hill.   When she knocked on the trap-door a
voice from within called, "Who?"

"Wolf-woman," she answered as politely as she
could, restraining her anger.

"Come down," said the voice, and hearing her
name the fifty young Deer-warriors — who had
carefully whetted their horns — stood ready.   The
door flew open, and she started down the ladder.
But as soon as she set her foot on the first rung,
all the Deer-people shouted:

"Look what feet!"   For, though the Deer is so
much larger than the Wolf, it has smaller feet.

At this she was very much ashamed, and pulled
back her foot; but soon her anger was stronger,
and she started down again.   But each time the

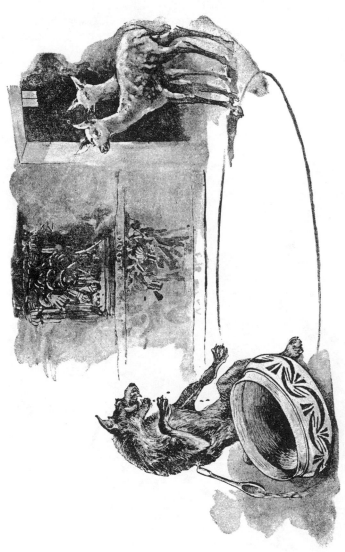

Deer-people laughed and shouted, and she drew back.

At last they were quiet, and she came down the ladder.   When she had told her story the old men of the Deer-people said :

"This is a serious case, and we must not judge it lightly.   Come, we will make an agreement. Let soup be brought, and we will eat together. And if you eat all your soup without spilling a drop, you shall have the Fawns."

"Ho!" thought the Wolf. "*That* is easy enough, for I will be very careful."   And aloud she said: "It is well.   Let us eat."

So a big bowl of soup was brought, and each took a *guayave* [1] and rolled it like a spoon to dip up the soup.   The old Wolf was very careful, and had almost finished her soup without spilling a drop. But just as she was lifting the last sup to her mouth the Fawns appeared suddenly in the door of the next room, and at sight of them she dropped the soup in her lap.

"She spilled!" shouted all the Deer-people, and the fifty chosen warriors rushed upon her and tore her to pieces with their sharp horns.

That was the end of the treacherous Wolf; and from that day the Wolf and the Deer have been enemies, and the Wolf is a little afraid of the Deer. And the two Fawns? Oh, they still live with the Deer-people in that black hill below Tomé.

[1] An Indian bread made by spreading successive films of blue corn-meal batter on a flat hot stone.   It looks more like a piece of wasp's nest than anything else, but is very good to eat.

XXVI

THE SOBBING PINE

ANOTHER folk-story told by the Quères colony in Isleta also relates to Acoma, perched upon the great round cliff in its far, fair valley.

Among the folk-lore heroes of whom every Quères lad has heard is Ees-tée-ah Muts, the Arrow Boy. He was a great hunter and did many remarkable things, but there was once a time when all his courage and strength were of no avail,—when but for the help of a little squirrel he would have perished miserably.

On reaching manhood Ees-tée-ah Muts married the daughter of the Kot-chin (chief). She was a very beautiful girl and her hunter-husband was very fond of her. But, alas! she was secretly a witch and every night when Ees-tée-ah Muts was asleep she used to fly away to the mountains, where the witches held their uncanny meetings. You must know that these witches have dreadful appetites, and that there is nothing in the world of which they are so fond as boiled baby.

Ees-tée-ah Muts, who was a very good man, had no suspicion that his wife was guilty of such practices, and she was very careful to keep him in ignorance of it.

One day, when the witch-wife was planning to go to a meeting, she stole a fat young baby and put it to cook in a great *olla* (earthen jar) in the dark inner room.   But before night she found she must go for water, and as the strange stone reservoir at Acoma is a laborious half-mile from the houses, she would be gone some time.   So, as she departed with a bright-painted *tinaja* upon her head, she charged her husband on no account to enter the inner room.

When she was gone Ees-tée-ah Muts began to ponder what she had said, and he feared that all was not well.   He went to the inner room and looked around, and when he found the baby cooking he was grieved, as any good husband would be, for then he knew that his wife was a witch. But when his wife returned with water, he said not a word, keeping only a sharp lookout to see what would come.

Very early that night Ees-tée-ah Muts pretended to go to sleep, but he was really very wide awake. His wife was quiet, but he could feel that she was watching him.   Presently a cat came sneaking into the room and whispered to the witch-wife :

"Why do you not come to the meeting, for we await you?"

"Wait me yet a little," she whispered, "until the man is sound asleep."

The cat crept away, and Ees-tée-ah Muts kept very still.   By and by an owl came in and bade the woman hurry.   And at last, thinking her hus-

band asleep, the witch-wife rose noiselessly and
went out. As soon as she was gone, Ees-tée-ah
Muts got up and followed her at a distance, for it
was a night of the full moon.

The witch-wife walked a long way till she came
to the foot of the Black Mesa, where was a great
dark hole with a rainbow in its mouth. As she
passed under the rainbow she turned herself into a
cat and disappeared within the cave. Ees-tée-ah
Muts crept softly up and peered in. He saw a
great firelit room full of witches in the shapes of
ravens and vultures, wolves and other animals of ill
omen. They were gathered about their feast and
were enjoying themselves greatly, eating and dancing and singing and planning evil to mankind.

For a long time Ees-tée-ah Muts watched them,
but at last one caught sight of his face peering in
at the hole.

"Bring him in!" shouted the chief witch, and
many of them rushed out and surrounded him and
dragged him into the cave.

"Now," said the chief witch, who was very angry,
"we have caught you as a spy and we ought to kill
you. But if you will save your life and be one
of us, go home and bring me the hearts of your
mother and sister, and I will teach you all our ways,
so that you shall be a mighty wizard."

Ees-tée-ah Muts hurried home to Acoma and
killed two sheep; for he knew, as every Indian
knows, that it was useless to try to escape from the
witches. Taking the hearts of the sheep, he
quickly returned to the chief witch, to whom he
gave them. But when the chief witch pricked the
hearts with a sharp stick they swelled themselves

out like a frog. Then he knew that he had been deceived, and was very angry, but pretending not to care he ordered Ees-tée-ah Muts to go home, which the frightened hunter was very glad to do.

But next morning when Ees-tée-ah Muts awoke he was not in his own home at all, but lying on a tiny shelf far up a dizzy cliff. To jump was certain death, for it was a thousand feet to the ground; and climb he could not, for the smooth rock rose a thousand feet above his head. Then he knew that he had been bewitched by the chief of those that have the evil road, and that he must die. He could hardly move without falling from the narrow shelf, and there he lay with bitter thoughts until the sun was high overhead.

At last a young Squirrel came running along the ledge, and, seeing him, ran back to its mother, crying:

"*Nana!* *Nana!* Here is a dead man lying on our ledge!"

"No, he is not dead," said the Squirrel-mother when she had looked, "but I think he is very hungry. Here, take this acorn-cup and carry him some corn-meal and water."

The young Squirrel brought the acorn-cup full of wet corn-meal, but Ees-tée-ah Muts would not take it, for he thought:

"Pah! What is so little when I am fainting for food?"

But the Squirrel-mother, knowing what was in his heart, said:

"Not so, *Sau-kée-ne* [friend]. It looks to be little, but there will be more than enough. Eat and be strong."

Still doubting, Ees-tée-ah Muts took the cup
and ate of the blue corn-meal until he could eat no
longer, and yet the acorn-cup was not empty.
Then the young Squirrel took the cup and brought
it full of water, and though he was very thirsty he
could not drain it.

"Now, friend," said the Squirrel-mother, when
he was refreshed by his meal, "you cannot yet
get down from here, where the witches put you;
but wait, for I am the one that will help you."

She went to her store-room and brought out a
pine-cone, which she dropped over the great cliff.
Ees-tée-ah Muts lay on the narrow ledge as
patiently as he could, sleeping sometimes and
sometimes thinking of his strange plight. Next
morning he could see a stout young pine-tree
growing at the bottom of the cliff, where he was
very sure there had been no tree at all the day
before. Before night it was a large tree, and the
second morning it was twice as tall. The young
Squirrel brought him meal and water in the acorn-
cup twice a day, and now he began to be confident
that he would escape.

By the evening of the fourth day the magic pine
towered far above his head, and it was so close to
the cliff that he could touch it from his shelf.

"Now, Friend Man," said the Squirrel-mother,
"follow me!" and she leaped lightly into the tree.
Ees-tée-ah Muts seized a branch and swung over
into the tree, and letting himself down from bough
to bough, at last reached the ground in safety.

The Squirrel-mother came with him to the
ground, and he thanked her for her kindness.

" But now I must go back to my home," she said. " Take these seeds of the pine-tree and these piñon-nuts which I have brought for you, and be very careful of them. When you get home, give your wife the pine-seeds, but you must eat the piñons. So now, good-by," and off she went up the tree.

When Ees-tée-ah Muts had come to Acoma and climbed the dizzy stone ladder and stood in the adobe town, he was very much surprised. For the four days of his absence had really been four years, and the people looked strange. All had given him up for dead, and his witch-wife had married another man, but still lived in the same house, which was hers.[1] When Ees-tée-ah Muts entered she seemed very glad to see him, and pretended to know nothing of what had befallen him. He said nothing about it, but talked pleasantly while he munched the piñon-nuts, giving her the pine-seeds to eat. Her new husband made a bed for Ees-tée-ah Muts, and in the morning very early the two men went away together on a hunt.

That afternoon the mother of the witch-wife went to visit her daughter, but when she came near the house she stopped in terror, for far up through the roof grew a great pine-tree, whose furry arms came out at doors and windows. That was the end of the witch-wife, for the magic seed had sprouted in her stomach, and she was turned into a great, sad Pine that swayed above her home, and moaned and sobbed forever, as all her Pine-children do to this day.

[1] It is one of the fundamental customs of the Pueblos that the house and its general contents belong to the wife ; the fields and other outside property to the husband.

XXVII

THE QUÈRES DIANA

THERE is a fragmentary Quères folk-story which bears internal evidence that its heroine was the mother of the Hero Twins — that is, the Moon. The adventure described here is one of those which befell the Moon-Mother, as related in several myths; though it has been varied, evidently by some later story-teller, and the identity of the heroine does not appear at first sight. It is a story common to all the Quères, and is undoubtedly ancient; but as I heard it first in Isleta its scene is laid in Laguna, a pueblo only two hundred years old.

Once upon a time the Tah-póh-pee[1] of Laguna had a daughter, who was the belle of the village. She was very fond of hunting, and killed as much game as any of the young men. Several miles south of Laguna is a very large sandstone dome rising in the plain, and in the heart of this rock the Governor's daughter had hollowed out a room in which she used to camp when on her hunting-expeditions.

One day there came a snow that covered the

[1] Governor.

ground so that one could easily track rabbits, and taking her bow and arrows she started off to hunt.

She had unusual luck, and by the time she reached the hunting-lodge she was loaded down with rabbits. The evening was very cold, and she was hungry; so, going into the rock-house, she built a fire on the hearth and began to roast a rabbit. Just as it was cooking a strong west wind came up and carried the savory smell from her chimney far to the east, till it reached a dark cavern in the Sandia Mountains, fifty miles away. There lived an old giantess, the terror of all the world, and when she caught a whiff of that sweet meat she started up and rubbed her big red eye.

"Um!" she cried, "that is good! I am going to see where it is, for I have had nothing to eat to-day."

In two steps she was at the rock-house, and, stooping down, she called at the door: "Quáhtzee? [How are you?] What are you cooking in there?"

"Rabbits," said the girl, dreadfully scared at that great voice.

"Then give me one," shouted the old giantess. The girl threw one out at the door, and the giantess swallowed it at a gulp and demanded more. The girl kept throwing them out until all were gone. Then the giantess called for her *manta* (dress), and her shawl and her buckskin leggings, and ate them all, and at last said:

"Little girl, now you come out, and let me eat you."

The girl began to cry bitterly when she saw that great savage eye at the door, which was so small that the giantess could not get her huge hand in. She repeated her commands thrice, and when the girl still refused to come out, picked up a great boulder and began to hammer the rock-house to pieces. But just as she had broken off the roof and stooped to pick out the girl, two hunters chanced to pass and hear the noise. They crept up and shot the giantess through the neck with their strong arrows and killed her, and, bringing new clothes for the girl, took her home safely to Kó-iks (the native name for Laguna), where she lived for many years.

XXVIII

A PUEBLO BLUEBEARD

ANOTHER fragmentary story of the Quères seems to refer to this same remarkable woman. You will see the connection when you remember that the Moon disappears every month; and I should judge that the following myth means that the Storm-King steals her.

Once upon a time a chief of Acoma had a lovely daughter. One day a handsome stranger stole her and took her away to his home, which was in the heart of the Snow Mountain (Mt. San Mateo). He was none other than Mast-Truan, one of the Storm-Gods. Bringing his captive home, the powerful stranger gave her the finest clothing and treated her very nicely. But most of the time he had to be away from home, attending to the storms, and she became very lonesome, for there was no one to keep her company but Mast-Truan's wrinkled old mother.

One day when she could stand the loneliness no longer, she decided to take a walk through the enormous house and look at the rooms which she had not seen. Opening a door she came into a very large room toward the east; and there were a lot of women crying and shivering with cold, for they had nothing to wear. Going through this room she came to another, which was full of gaunt, starving women, and here and there one lay dead upon the floor; and in the next room were scores of bleached and ghastly skeletons. And this was what Mast-Truan did with his wives when he was tired of them. The girl saw her fate, and, returning to her room, sat down and wept—but there was no escape, for Mast-Truan's old hag of a mother forever guarded the outer door.

When Mast-Truan came home again, his wife said: "It is now long that I have not seen my fathers. Let me go home for a little while."

"Well," said he, "here is some corn which must be shelled. When you have shelled it and ground it, I will let you out"; and he showed her four great rooms piled from floor to ceiling with ears of corn. It was more than one could shell in a year; and when her husband went out, she sat down again to cry and bemoan her fate.

Just then a queer little old woman appeared before her, with a kindly smile. It was a *cumúsh-quio* (fairy-woman).

"What is the matter, my daughter?" asked the old fairy, gently, "and why do you weep?"

The captive told her all, and the fairy said: "Do not fear, daughter, for I will help you, and we will have all the corn shelled and ground in four days."

So they fell to work. For two days the girl kept shelling; and though she could not see the old fairy at all, she could always hear at her side the click of the ears together. Then for two days she kept grinding on her *metate*, apparently alone, but hearing the constant grind of another *metate* close beside her.   At the end of the fourth day the last kernel had been scrubbed into blue meal, and she was very happy.   Then the old fairy-woman appeared again, bringing a large basket and a rope. She opened the doors to all the rooms where the poor women were prisoners, and bade them all get into the basket one by one.   Mast-Truan had taken away the ladder from the house when he left, that no one might be able to get out; but with her basket and rope the good old fairy-woman let them all down to the ground, and told them to hurry home—which they did as fast as ever their poor, starved legs could carry them.   Then the fairy-woman and the girl escaped, and made their way to Acoma.   So there was a Moon again—and that it *was* the Moon, we may be very sure; since this same girl became the mother of the Hero Twins, who were assuredly Children of the Moon.

XXIX

THE HERO TWINS

THAT the heroes of "The Magic Hide-and-Seek" were really the Pueblo Castor and Pollux, the twin offspring of the Sun-Father and the Moon-Mother, is more than probable. For some reason which I do not know, these demigods do not figure as clearly in the Tée-wahn myths as among the other Pueblos, the Navajos and the Apaches; but that they are believed in, even in Isleta, there can be no doubt. They were the ones who led mankind forth from its first home in the dark center of the earth.[1] The rainbow is their bow, the lightnings are their arrows. Among the other Pueblos there are countless folk-stories about these Hero Twins; and the following example myth will quickly remind you of the boys who played hide-and-seek. It is told in Isleta, though I have never heard it from the Tée-wahn people there. Ever since the great drouth of a generation ago, about one hundred and fifty Quères, starved out from the pueblos of Acoma and Laguna, have dwelt in Isleta, and they are now a

[1] They are represented in the sacred dances by the Káh-pee-óo-nin, " the Dying-of-Cold" (because they are always naked except for the breech-clout).

permanent part of the village, recognized by representation in the civil and religious government, though speaking an altogether different language. Tée-wahn and Quères cannot understand each other in their own tongues, so they have to communicate in Spanish.

Máw-Sahv and Oó-yah-wee, as the Hero Twins are named in Quères, had the Sun for a father. Their mother died when they were born, and lay lifeless upon the hot plain. But the two wonderful boys, as soon as they were a minute old, were big and strong, and began playing.

There chanced to be in a cliff to the southward a nest of white crows; and presently the young crows said: "*Nana*, what is that over there? Is n't it two babies?"

"Yes," replied the Mother-Crow, when she had taken a look. "Wait and I will bring them." So she brought the boys safely, and then their dead mother; and, rubbing a magic herb on the body of the latter, soon brought her to life.

By this time Máw-Sahv and Oó-yah-wee were sizable boys, and the mother started homeward with them.

"Now," said she when they reached the edge of the valley and could look across to that wondrous rock whereon stands Acoma, "go to yonder town, my sons, for that is Ah-ko, where live your grandfather and grandmother, my parents; and I will wait here. Go ye in at the west end of the town and stand at the south end of the council-grounds until some one speaks to you; and ask them to take you to the Cacique, for he is your grandfather.

You will know his house, for the ladder to it has three uprights instead of two. When you go in and tell your story, he will ask you a question to see if you are really his grandchildren, and will give you four chances to answer what he has in a bag in the corner. No one has ever been able to guess what is in it, but there are birds."

The Twins did as they were bidden, and presently came to Acoma and found the house of the old Cacique. When they entered and told their story, he said: "Now I will try you. What is in yonder bag?"

"A rattlesnake," said the boys.

"No," said the Cacique, "it is not a rattlesnake. Try again."

"Birds," said the boys.

"Yes, they are birds. Now I know that you are truly my grandchildren, for no one else could ever guess." And he welcomed them gladly, and sent them back with new dresses and jewelry to bring their mother.

When she was about to arrive, the Twins ran ahead to the house and told her father, mother, and sister to leave the house until she should enter; but not knowing what was to come, they would not go out. When she had climbed the big ladder to the roof and started down through the trap-door by the room-ladder, her sister cried out with joy at seeing her, and she was so startled that she fell from the ladder and broke her neck, and never could be brought to life again.

Máw-Sahv and Oó-yah-wee grew up to astounding adventures and achievements. While still

very young in years, they did very remarkable
things; for they had a miraculously rapid growth,
and at an age when other boys were toddling
about home, these Hero Twins had already become very famous hunters and warriors. They
were very fond of stories of adventure, like less
precocious lads; and after the death of their
mother they kept their grandmother busy telling
them strange tales. She had a great many an-
ecdotes of a certain ogre-giantess who lived in the
dark gorges of the mountains to the South, and so
much did Máw-Sahv and Oó-yah-wee hear of this
wonderful personage — who was the terror of all
that country — that their boyish ambition was fired.

One day when their grandmother was busy they
stole away from home with their bows and arrows,
and walked miles and miles, till they came to a
great forest at the foot of the mountain. In the
edge of it sat the old Giant-woman, dozing in the
sun, with a huge basket beside her. She was so
enormous and looked so fierce that the boys' hearts
stood still, and they would have hidden, but just
then she caught sight of them, and called: "Come,
little boys, and get into this basket of mine, and I
will take you to my house."

"Very well," said Máw-Sahv, bravely hiding his
alarm. "If you will take us through this big
forest, which we would like to see, we will go with
you."

The Giant-woman promised, and the lads
clambered into her basket, which she took upon
her back and started off. As she passed through
the woods, the boys grabbed lumps of pitch from the

14

tall pines and smeared it all over her head and back so softly that she did not notice it. Once she sat down to rest, and the boys slyly put a lot of big stones in the basket, set fire to her pitched hair, and hurriedly climbed a tall pine.

Presently the Giant-woman got up and started on toward home; but in a minute or two her head and *manta* were all of a blaze. With a howl that shook the earth, she dropped the basket and rolled on the ground, grinding her great head into the sand until she at last got the fire extinguished. But she was badly scorched and very angry, and still angrier when she looked in the basket and found only a lot of stones. She retraced her steps until she found the boys hidden in the pine-tree, and said to them: "Come down, children, and get into my basket, that I may take you to my house, for now we are almost there."

The boys, knowing that she could easily break down the tree if they refused, came down. They got into the basket, and soon she brought them to her home in the mountain. She set them down upon the ground and said: "Now, boys, go and bring me a lot of wood, that I may make a fire in the oven and bake you some sweet cakes."

The boys gathered a big pile of wood, with which she built a roaring fire in the adobe oven outside the house. Then she took them and washed them very carefully, and taking them by the necks, thrust them into the glowing oven and sealed the door with a great, flat rock, and left them there to be roasted.

But the Trues were friends of the Hero Twins,

and did not let the heat harm them at all. When the old Giant-woman had gone into the house, Máw-Sahv and Oó-yah-wee broke the smaller stone that closed the smoke-hole of the oven, and crawled out from their fiery prison unsinged. They ran around and caught snakes and toads and gathered up dirt and dropped them down into the oven through the smoke-hole; and then, watching when the Giant-woman's back was turned, they sneaked into the house and hid in a huge *olla* on the shelf.

Very early in the morning the Giant-woman's baby began to cry for some boy-meat. "Wait till it is well cooked," said the mother; and hushed the child till the sun was well up. Then she went out and unsealed the oven, and brought in the sad mess the boys had put there. "They have cooked away to almost nothing," she said; and she and the Giant-baby sat down to eat. "Is n't this nice?" said the baby; and Máw-Sahv could not help saying, "You nasty things, to like that!"

"Eh? Who is that?" cried the Giant-woman, looking around till she found the boys hidden in the *olla*. So she told them to come down, and gave them some sweet cakes, and then sent them out to bring her some more wood.

It was evening when they returned with a big load of wood, which Máw-Sahv had taken pains to get green. He had also picked up in the mountains a long, sharp splinter of quartz.[1] The evening was cool, and they built a big fire in the fireplace. But immediately, as the boys had planned,

1 A thunder-knife.

the green wood began to smoke at a dreadful rate, and soon the room was so dense with it that they all began to cough and strangle. The Giant-woman got up and opened the window and put her head out for a breath of fresh air; and Máw-Sahv, pulling out the white-hot splinter of quartz from the fire, stabbed her in the back so that she died. Then they killed the Giant-baby, and at last felt that they were safe.

Now the Giant-woman's house was a very large one, and ran far back into the very heart of the mountain. Having got rid of their enemies, the Hero Twins decided to explore the house; and, taking their bows and arrows, started boldly down into the deep, dark rooms. After traveling a long way in the dark, they came to a huge room in which corn and melons and pumpkins were growing abundantly. On and on they went, till at last they heard the growl of distant thunder. Following the sound, they came presently to a room in the solid rock, wherein the lightning was stored. Going in, they took the lightning and played with it awhile, throwing it from one to the other, and at last started home, carrying their strange toy with them.

When they reached Acoma and told their grand-mother of their wonderful adventures, she held up her withered old hands in amazement. And she was nearly scared to death when they began to play with the lightning, throwing it around the house as though it had been a harmless ball, while the thunder rumbled till it shook the great rock of Acoma. They had the blue lightning which belongs in the West; and the yellow lightning of the

North; and the red lightning of the East; and the white lightning of the South; and with all these they played merrily.

But it was not very long till Shée-wo-nah, the Storm-King, had occasion to use the lightning; and when he looked in the room where he was wont to keep it, and found it gone, his wrath knew no bounds. He started out to find who had stolen it; and passing by Acoma he heard the thunder as the Hero Twins were playing ball with the lightning. He pounded on the door and ordered them to give him his lightning, but the boys refused. Then he summoned the storm, and it began to rain and blow fearfully outside; while within the boys rattled their thunder in loud defiance, regardless of their grandmother's entreaties to give the Storm-King his lightning.

It kept raining violently, however, and the water came pouring down the chimney until the room was nearly full, and they were in great danger of drowning. But luckily for them, the Trues were still mindful of them; and just in the nick of time sent their servant, Teé-oh-pee, the Badger, who is the best of diggers, to dig a hole up through the floor; all the water ran out, and they were saved. And so the Hero Twins outwitted the Storm-King.

South of Acoma, in the pine-clad gorges and mesas, the world was full of Bears. There was one old She-Bear in particular, so huge and fierce that all men feared her; and not even the boldest hunter dared go to the south—for there she had her home with her two sons.

Máw-sahv and Oó-yah-wee were famous hunters, and always wished to go south; but their
grandmother always forbade them.   One day,
however, they stole away from the house, and got
into the cañon.   At last they came to the She-
Bear's house; and there was old Quée-ah asleep
in front of the door.   Máw-sahv crept up very
carefully and threw in her face a lot of ground
chile,[1] and ran.   At that the She-Bear began to
sneeze, *ah-hútch! ah-hútch!*   She could not stop,
and kept making *ah-hútch* until she sneezed herself to death.

Then the Twins took their thunder-knives and
skinned her.   They stuffed the great hide with
grass, so that it looked like a Bear again, and tied
a buckskin rope around its neck.

"Now," said Máw-sahv, "We will give our
grandma a trick!"

So, taking hold of the rope, they ran toward
Acoma, and the Bear came behind them as if leaping.   Their grandmother was going for water;
and from the top of the cliff she saw them running
so in the valley, and the Bear jumping behind
them.   She ran to her house and painted one side
of her face black with charcoal, and the other side
red with the blood of an animal;[2] and, taking a bag
of ashes, ran down the cliff and out at the Bear, to
make it leave the boys and come after her.

But when she saw the trick, she reproved the
boys for their rashness — but in her heart she was
very proud of them.

---

1 The fiery red-pepper of the Southwest.
2 Ancient tokens of mourning.

XXX

THE HUNGRY GRANDFATHERS

A DISOBEDIENT child is something I have never seen among the Pueblos, in all the years I have lived with them. The parents are very kind, too. My little *amigos* in Isleta and the other Pueblo towns — for they are my friends in all — are never spoiled ; but neither are they punished much.[1] Personal acquaintance with a spanking is what very few of them have. The idea of obedience is inborn and inbred. A word is generally enough ; and for extreme cases it only needs the threat: " Look out, or I will send for the Grandfathers ! "

Now, perhaps you do not know who the Grandfathers are ; but every Pueblo youngster does. It has nothing to do with the " truly " grandpa, who is as lovely an institution among the Tée-wahn as anywhere else. No, the *Abuelos* were of an altogether different sort. That name is Spanish, and has three applications in Isleta: real grandparents ; the remarkable masked officials of a certain dance ; and the bad Old Ones. These last

---

[1] I must qualify this now. In the last two years I have seen one spoiled child — just one, in ten years' acquaintance with 9000 Pueblos !

are called in the Tée-wahn tongue *T'ai-kár-nin*
(Those-Who-Eat-People). They were, in fact, aboriginal Ogres, who once sadly ravaged Isleta.

The *T'ai-kár-nin* had no town, but dwelt in
caves of the lava mountain a couple of miles west
of this village — the *Kú-mai* hill. It is a bad
place at best: bleak, black, rough, and forbidding
— just the place that a properly constituted Ogre
would choose for his habitation. In the first place,
it is to the west of the town, which is "bad medicine" in itself to any Indian, for that point of the
compass belongs to the dead and to bad spirits.
Then its color is against it; and, still worse, it is to
this day the common stamping-ground of all the
witches in this part of the country, where they
gather at night for their diabolical caucuses. Of
its serious disrepute I can convey no better idea
to the enlightened and superstitionless American
mind than by saying that it is a sort of aboriginal
"haunted house."

So the hill of *Kú-mai* was a peculiarly fit place
for the Ogres to dwell in. Deep in its gloomy
bowels they huddled on the white sand which floors
all the caves there; and crannies overhead carried
away the smoke from their fires, which curled from
crevices at the top of the peak far above them.
Ignorant Americans would probably have taken it
for a volcanic emission; but the good people of
Shee-eh-whíb-bak knew better.

These Ogres were larger than ordinary men,
but otherwise carried no outward sign of their odi-
ous calling. Their teeth were just like anybody's
good teeth, and they had neither "tushes" nor

horns nor hoofs.   Indeed, except for their unusual
size, they would have been easily mistaken for
Indians of some distant tribe.   But, *ay de mi!*
How strong they were!   One could easily whip
five common men in a bunch — "men even as
strong as my son, Francisco," says Desiderio; and
Francisco is as stout as a horse.

They were people of very fastidious palates,
these Ogres.   Nothing was good enough for them
except human flesh — and young at that.   Their
fare was entirely baby — baby young, baby brown,
and baby very fat.   They never molested the
adults ; but as often as they found an appetite they
descended upon the village, scooped up what children they could lay their hands upon, and carried
them off to their caves.   There they had enormous
ollas, into which half a dozen children could be
thrown at once.

There seemed to be some spell about these
Ogres — besides their frequent hungry spells — for
the Pueblos, who were so brave in the face of other
foes, never dared fight these terrible cave-dwellers.
They continued to devastate the village, until
babies were at a premium, and few to be had at
any price; and the only way the people dared to
try to circumvent them was by strategy.   In time
it came about that every house where there were
children, or a reasonable hope of them, had secret
cubby-holes back of the thick adobe walls; with
little doors which shut flush with the wall and were
also plastered with adobe, so that when they were
shut a stranger — even if he were a sharp-eyed
Indian — would never dream of their existence.

And whenever arose the dreaded cry, " Here come the *T'ai-kár-nin!* " the children were hustled, shivering and noiseless, into the secret recesses, and the doors were shut. Then Mr. Ogre could come in and peer and sniff about as he liked, but no chance to fill his market-basket could he find. And when parents were forced to go away and leave the babies behind, the poor young ones were inclosed in their safe but gloomy prisons, and there in darkness and silence had to await the parental home-coming. These inconveniences were gladly borne, however, since they preserved the children — and we all know that preserved baby is better than baby-stew. It was, of course, rather rough on the Ogres, who began to find all their belts most distressfully loose; but no one seemed to consider their feelings. They were pretty well starved when the Spaniards came and delivered the suffering Isleteños by driving off these savage neighbors. This looks suspiciously as if the whole myth of the Ogres had sprung from the attacks of the cruel Apaches and Navajos in the old days.

There was one queer thing about these Ogres — on their forages they always wore buckskin masks, just like those of the *Abuelos* of the sacred dance. Their bare faces were seen sometimes by hunters who encountered them on the *llano*, but never here in town. It was in connection with these masks that Isleta had a great sensation recently. The Hungry Grandfathers had been almost forgotten, except as a word to change the minds of children who had about quarter of a mind to be naughty; but interest was revived by a dis-

covery of which my venerable friend Desiderio
Peralta was the hero.

This dear old man—news of his death has come
to me as I write this very chapter—was a remarkable character. He was one of "the oldest inhabitants" of New Mexico—older than any other
Indian among the twelve hundred of Isleta, except
tottering Diego; and that is saying a great deal.
His hair was very gray, and his kindly old face
such an incredible mass of wrinkles that I used to
fancy Father Time himself must have said: "No,
no! You apprentices never do a thing right!
Here, *this* is the way to put on wrinkles!" and that
he then and there took old Desiderio for a model,
and showed the journeymen wrinkle-makers a trick
they never dreamed of. Certainly the job was never
so well done before. From chin to hair-roots,
from ear to ear, was such a crowded, tangled, in-
extricable maze of furrows and cross-harrow lines as
I firmly believe never dwelt together on any other
one human face. Why, Desiderio could have furnished an army of old men with wrinkles! I never
saw him smile without fearing that some of those
wrinkles were going to fall off the edge, so crowded were they at best!

But if his face was *arrugada*, his brain was not.
He was bright and chipper as a young blackbird,
and it was only of late that a touch of rheumatism
took the youth out of his legs. Until recently he
held the important position of Captain of War
for the pueblo; and only two years ago I had the
pleasure of going with two hundred *other* Indians
on a huge rabbit-hunt which was under his per-

sonal supervision, and in which he was as active as
any one, both on his feet and with the unerring
boomerang. His eyes were good to find about as
much through the sights of a rifle as anybody's;
and on the whole he was worth a good deal more
than I expect to be some seventy years from now.
He was a good neighbor, too; and I had few
pleasanter hours than those spent in talking with
this genial old shrivel, who was *muy sabio* in all
the folk-lore and wisdom of his unfathomable race;
and very close-mouthed about it, too—as they all
are. Still, there were some things which he seemed
willing to confide to me; and he always had an attentive listener.

Desiderio was not yet too old to herd his own
cattle during the season when they roam abroad;
and, while thus engaged, he made a discovery
which set the whole quiet village agog, though
no other outsider ever heard of it.

One day in 1889 Desiderio started out from the
village, driving his cattle. Having steered them
across the *acequia* and up the sand-hills to the beginning of the plain, he climbed to the top of the
Kú-mai to watch them through the day—as has
been the custom of Isleta herders from time imme-
morial. In wandering over the rocky top of the
peak, he came to a ledge of rocks on the southeast
spur of the hill; and there found a fissure, at one
end of which was a hole as large as a man's head.
Desiderio put his face and his wrinkles down to
the hole to see what he could see; and all was
dark inside. But if his eyes strained in vain, his
ears did not. From far down in the bowels of the

mountain came a strange roaring, as of a heavy wind. Desiderio was somewhat dismayed at this; for he knew at once that he had found one of the chimneys of the Ogres; but he did not run away. Hunting around awhile, he found in the fissures of the rocks some ancient buckskin masks—the very ones worn by the Ogres, of course. He put them back, and coming to town straightway told the medicine-men of the Black Eyes—one of the two parties here. They held a *junta;* and after mature deliberation decided to go and get the masks. This was done, and the masks are now treasured in the Black Eye medicine-house.

I have several times carefully explored the *Kú-mai*—a difficult and tiresome task, thanks to the knife-like lava fragments which cover it everywhere, and which will cut a pair of new strong shoes to pieces in an afternoon. It is true that in this hill of bad repute there are several lava-caves, with floors of white sand blown in from the *llano;* and that in these caves there are a few human bones. No doubt some of the savage nomads camped or lived there. None of those famous *ollas* are visible; nor have I ever been able to find any other relics of the Hungry Grandfathers.

XXXI

ALL the animals with which the Tée-wahn are familiar—the buffalo (which they used to hunt on the vast plains to the eastward), the bear, deer, antelope, mountain lion, badger, wild turkey, fox, eagle, crow, buzzard, rabbit, and so on—appear in their legends and fairy tales, as well as in their religious ceremonials and beliefs. Too-wháy-deh, the Coyote,[1] or little prairie wolf, figures in countless stories, and always to his own disadvantage. Smart as he is in some things, he believes whatever is told him; and by his credulity becomes the butt of all the other animals, who never tire of "April-fooling" him. He is also a great coward. To call an Indian here "*Too-wháy-deh*" is one of the bitterest insults that can be offered him.

[1] Pronounced Coy-óh-ty.

You have already heard how the Coyote fared at the hands of the fun-loving Bear, and of the Crows and the Blackbirds. A very popular tale is that of his adventure with a bright cousin of his.

Once upon a time Too-wháy-shur-wée-deh, the Little-Blue-Fox,[1] was wandering near a pueblo, and chanced to come to the threshing-floors, where a great many crows were hopping. Just then the Coyote passed, very hungry; and while yet far off, said: "Ai! how the stomach cries! I will just eat Little-Blue-Fox." And coming, he said:

"Now, Little-Blue-Fox, you have troubled me enough! You are the cause of my being chased by the dogs and people, and now I will pay you. I am going to eat you up this very now!"

"No, Coyote-friend," answered the Little-Blue-Fox, "*don't* eat me up! I am here guarding these chickens, for there is a wedding in yonder house, which is my master's, and these chickens are for the wedding-dinner. Soon they will come for the chickens, and will invite me to the dinner—and you can come also."

"Well," said the Coyote, "if *that* is so, I will not eat you, but will help you watch the chickens." So he lay down beside him.

At this, Little-Blue-Fox was troubled, thinking how to get away; and at last he said:

"Friend Too-wháy-deh, I make strange that they have not before now come for the chickens. Perhaps they have forgotten. The best way is for

1 He is always a hero, and as smart as the Coyote is stupid. His beautiful pelt is an important part of the costume worn in many of the sacred dances of the Tée-wahn.

me to go to the house and see what the servants are doing."

"It is well," said the Coyote. "Go, then, and I will guard the chickens for you."

So the Little-Blue-Fox started toward the house; but getting behind a small hill, he ran away with fast feet. When it was a good while, and he did not come back, the Coyote thought: "While he is gone, I will give myself some of the chickens." Crawling up on his belly to the threshing-floor, he gave a great leap. But the chickens were only crows, and they flew away. Then he began to say evil of the Little-Blue-Fox for giving him a trick, and started on the trail, vowing: "I will eat him up wherever I catch him."

After many miles he overtook the Little-Blue-Fox, and with a bad face said: "Here! Now I am going to eat you up!"

The other made as if greatly excited, and answered: "No, friend Coyote! Do you not hear that *tombé*[1]?"

The Coyote listened, and heard a drum in the pueblo.

"Well," said the Little-Blue-Fox, "I am called for that dance,[2] and very soon they will come for me. Won't you go too?"

"If that is so, I will not eat you, but we will go to the dance." And the Coyote sat down and began to comb his hair and to make himself pretty with face-paint. When no one came, the Little-Blue-Fox said:

[1] Pronounced tom-báy. The sacred drum used in Pueblo dances.
[2] In all such Indian dances the participants are named by the officials.

"THERE THEY STOOD SIDE BY SIDE."

"Friend Coyote, I make strange that the *al-guazil* does not come. It is best for me to go up on this hill, whence I can see into the village. You wait here."

"He will not dare to give me another trick," thought the Coyote. So he replied: "It is well. But do not forget to call me."

So the Little-Blue-Fox went up the hill; and as soon as he was out of sight, he began to run for his life.

Very long the Coyote waited; and at last, being tired, went up on the hill — but there was no one there. Then he was very angry, and said: "I will follow him, and eat him surely! *Nothing* shall save him!" And finding the trail, he began to follow as fast as a bird.

Just as the Little-Blue-Fox came to some high cliffs, he looked back and saw the Coyote coming over a hill. So he stood up on his hind feet and put his fore paws up against the cliff, and made many groans, and was as if much excited. In a moment came the Coyote, very angry, crying: "Now you shall not escape me! I am going to eat you up now — now!"

"Oh, no, friend Too-wháy-deh!" said the other; "for I saw this cliff falling down, and ran to hold it up. If I let go, it will fall and kill us both. But come, help me to hold it."

Then the Coyote stood up and pushed against the cliff with his fore paws, very hard; and there they stood side by side.

Time passing so, the Little-Blue-Fox said:

"Friend Too-wháy-deh, it is long that I am

holding up the cliff, and I am very tired and thirsty.
You are fresher.   So you hold up the cliff while I
go and hunt water for us both; for soon you too
will be thirsty.   There is a lake somewhere on the
other side of this mountain; I will find it and get a
drink, and then come back and hold up the cliff
while you go."

The Coyote agreed, and the Little-Blue-Fox
ran away over the mountain till he came to the
lake, just as the moon was rising.

But soon the Coyote was very tired and thirsty,
for he held up the cliff with all his might.   At last
he said: "Ai! how hard it is!   I am so thirsty
that I will go to the lake, even if I die!"

So he began to let go of the cliff, slowly, slowly—
until he held it only with his finger-nails; and then
he made a great jump away backward, and ran as
hard as he could to a hill.   But when he looked
around and saw that the cliff did not fall, he was
very angry, and swore to eat Too-wháy-shur-wée-
deh the very minute he should catch him.

Running on the trail, he came to the lake; and
there the Little-Blue-Fox was lying on the bank,
whining as if greatly excited.   "Now I *will* eat you
up, this minute!" cried the Coyote.   But the other
said: "No, Friend Too-wháy-deh!   Don't eat *me*
up!   I am waiting for some one who can swim as
well as you can.   I just bought a big cheese[1] from
a shepherd to share with you; but when I went to
drink, it slipped out of my hands into the water.

[1] Of course chickens and cheeses were not known to the Pueblos before the
Spanish conquest; and the cheese is so vital a part of the story that I hardly
think it can be an interpolation.   So this tale, though very old, is probably
not ancient—that is, it has been invented since 1600.

"'HOW SHALL I GET IT?' SAID THE COYOTE."

Come here, and I will show you." He took the Coyote to the edge of the high bank, and pointed to the moon in the water.

"M—m!" said the Coyote, who was fainting with hunger. "But how shall I get it? It is very deep in the water, and I shall float up before I can dive to it."

"That is true, friend," said the other. "There is but one way. We must tie some stones to your neck, to make you heavy so you can go down to it."

So they hunted about until they found a buck-skin thong and some large stones; and the Little-Blue-Fox tied the stones to the Coyote's neck, the Coyote holding his chin up, to help.

"Now, friend Too-wháy-deh, come here to the edge of the bank and stand ready. I will take you by the back and count *weem, wée-si, p'áh-chu!* And when I say *three*, you must jump and I will push—for now you are very heavy."

So he took the Coyote by the back of the neck, swaying him back and forth as he counted. And at "*p'áh-chu!*" he pushed hard, and the Coyote jumped, and went into the deep water, and— never came out again!

XXXII

DOCTOR FIELD-MOUSE

IT was the evening of the 14th of March. In the valley of the Rio Grande, that stands at the end of the winter. Now it is to open the big mother-canal that comes from the river to all the fields, giving them to drink after their long thirst; and now to plow the *milpas*, and to uncover the buried grape-vines, and make ready for the farmer's work.

As the door opened to admit stalwart Francisco to the big flickering room where we were all sitting in silence, the long, shrill wail of a Coyote, away up on the Accursed Hill, blew in after him on the boisterous March wind. The boys pricked up their ears; and bright-faced Manuelito[1] turned to his white-headed grandfather, and said:

"*Tata*, why is it that Too-wháy-deh always howls so? Perhaps he has a pain; for he has been crying ever since the beginning of the world —as they told us in the story of the Fawns and the She-Wolf."

"What, Unknowing!" answered the old man, kindly. "Hast thou never heard of the Coyote's

[1] Pronounced Mahn-way-lée-to.

toothache, and who was the first medicine-man in all the world? It is not well not to know that; for from that comes all that we know to cure the sick. And for that, I will tell—but it is the last story of the year. For to-morrow is *Tu-shée-wim*, the Spring Medicine-Dance; and the snakes are coming out from their winter houses. After that, we must not tell of the Things of Old. For it is very long ago; and if one made a mistake in telling, and said that which was not all true, *Ch'áh-rah-ráh-deh* would bite him, and he would die.[1] But this one I will tell thee."

In the First Days, when the people had broken through the crust of the earth, and had come up out of their dark prison, underground, and crossed Shee-p'ah-póon, the great Black Lake of Tears, they came to the shore on this side. Then it came that all the animals were made; and very soon the Coyote was sent by the Trues to carry a buckskin bag far south, and not to open it until he should come to the Peak of the White Clouds. For many days he ran south, with the bag on his back. But there was nothing to eat, and he grew very hungry. At last he thought: "Perhaps in this bag there is to eat." So he took it from his back, and untied the thongs, and looked in. But there was nothing in it except the stars; and as soon as the bag was opened they all flew up into the sky, where they are to this day.

[1] A fixed belief among the Pueblos, who will tell none of their myths between the Spring Medicine-Making, in March, and the Fall Medicine-Making, in October, lest the rattlesnake punish them for some slip from the truth.

When the Trues saw that Too-wháy-deh had disobeyed, they were angry, and made it that his punishment should be to wander up and down forever, howling with the toothache and finding no rest.

So Too-wháy-deh went out with his toothache, running all over the world groaning and crying; and when the other four-feet slept he could only sit and howl. Because he came to talk with the other animals, if they could not cure him, they caught the toothache too; and that is the reason why they sometimes cry. But none have it like the Coyote, who can find no rest.

In those times there were no medicine-men in the world,— not even of the people,— and the animals found no cure.

Time passing so, it came one day that T'hoo-chée-deh, the smallest of Mice, who lives in the little mounds around the chapparo-bush, was making his road underground, when he came to a kind of root with a sweet smell. T'hoo-chée-deh was very wise; and he took the root, and put it with others in a buckskin pouch he carried under his left arm.

In a few days Kee-oo-ée-deh, the Prairie-Dog, came with his head all fat with toothache, and said:

"Friend Field-Mouse, can you not cure me of this pain? For all say you are very wise with herbs."

"I do not know," answered T'hoo-chée-deh. "But we will try. For I have found a new root, and perhaps it is good."

So he mixed it with other roots, all pounded, and put it on the cheek of Kee-oo-ée-deh; and in a little, the toothache was gone.

In that time it was that there was so much

toothache among the animals that the Mountain
Lion, Commander of Beasts, called a council to
see what should be done.   When every kind that
walks on the ground had met, he asked each of
them if they had found no cure; but none of them
knew any.   The Coyote was there, howling with
pain; but all the other sick were at home.

At last it was to the Field-Mouse, who is the
smallest of all animals, and who did not wish to
seem wise until all the greater ones had spoken.
When the Mountain Lion said, "And thou, T'hoo-
chée-deh—hast thou a cure?" he rose in his place
and came forward modestly, saying: "If the others will allow me, and with the help of the Trues,
I will try what I found last."

Then he drew from his left-hand bag the roots
one by one; and last of all, the root of the *chee-
ma-hár,* explaining what it had done for Kee-oo-
ée-deh.   He pounded it to powder with a stone,
and mixed it with fat; and spreading it on flat
leaves, put it to the Coyote's jaw.   And in a little
the pain was gone.[1]

At that the Mountain Lion, the Bear, the Buffalo, and all the other Captains of Four-feet, de-
clared T'hoo-chée-deh the Father-of-All-Medicine.
They made a strong law that from that time the
body of the Field-Mouse should be held sacred, so
that no animal dares to kill him or even to touch him
dead.   And so it remains to this day.   But only the

[1] This cure is still practised among the Tée-wahn. The sovereign remedy
for toothache, however, is to go to the *estufa* after dark, carrying food in the
left hand, march round inside the big circular room three times, leave the
food under the secret recess in the wall where the scalps taken in old wars are
kept, and then come out. The toothache is always left behind!

birds and the snakes, who were not at the Council of the Four-feet, they do not respect T'hoo-chée-deh.

So the Field-Mouse was the first medicine-man. He chose one of each kind of four-feet to be his assistants, and taught them the use of all herbs, and how to cure pain, so that each might practise among his own people — a Bear-doctor for the Bears, and a Wolf-doctor for the Wolves, and so to all the tribes of the animals.

Of those he taught, there was one who was not a True Believer — the Badger. But he listened also, and made as if he believed all. With time, the teaching was done; and T'hoo-chée-deh sent all his assistant doctors home to their own peoples to heal. But whenever one of them was asked with the sacred corn-meal[1] to come and cure a sick one, he always came first to get the Father, the Field-Mouse, to accompany and help him.

But all this time Kahr-naí-deh, the Badger, was not believing; and at last he said to his wife:

" Now I will *see* if Old T'hoo-chée-deh is really a medicine-man. If he finds me, I will believe him."

So from that day for four days the Badger touched no food, until he was almost dead. And on the fifth day he said:

" *In-hlee-oo wáy-ee*, wife of me, go now and call T'hoo-chée-deh, to see if he will cure me."

So the Badger-wife went with meal to the house of the Field-Mouse, making to be very sad; and brought him back with her. When they came, the Badger was as if very sick and in great pain.

[1] The necessary accompaniment, among the Pueblos, of a call for the doctor. In some cases, the sacred smoking-herb was used. Either article was wrapped in corn-husk. See, also, "Some Strange Corners of Our Country," chapters xviii and xx.

T'hoo-chée-deh asked nothing; but took off the little pouch of roots and laid it beside him. And then rubbing a little wood-ashes on his hands, he put them on the stomach and breast of the Badger, rubbing and feeling. When he had felt the Badger's stomach, he began to sing:

Káhr-nah-hlóo-hlee wee-end-t'hú
Beh-hú hoo-báhn,
Ah-náh káh-chah-him-aí
T'hóo-chee-hlóo-hlee t'oh-ah-yin-áhb
Wee-end-t'hú beh-hú hoo-báhn.

(Badger-Old-Man four days
Has the hunger-killing,
To know, to know surely
If Field-Mouse-Old-Man
Has the Medicine Power.
Four days, four days,
He has the hunger-killing.)

When he had finished rubbing and singing, he said to the Badger:
"There is no need of a remedy. In my teaching I found you attentive—now be true. You have wasted, in trying my power. Now get up and eat, to make up for the lost. And do not think that way again."

With that, he took his pouch of roots and went home. As soon as he was out of the house, the Badger said to his wife:
"My wife, now I believe that Mouse-Old-Man *has* the Power; and never again will I think *that* way."

Then the Badger-wife brought food, and he ate—for he was dying of hunger. When he had eaten, the animals came in to see him, for they had heard that he was very sick. He told them all

that had been, and how T'hoo-chée-deh had known
his trick.   At that, all the animals were afraid of
the Field-Mouse, and respected him more than ever
— for it was plain that he indeed had the Power.

Time passing so, it came that one day the Men
of the Old made *nah-kú-ah-shu*, the great round-
hunt.   When they had made a great circle on the
llano, and killed many rabbits, some of them found
T'hoo-chée-deh, and made him prisoner.   They
brought him before the *principales*, who questioned
him, saying:

"How do you gain your life?"

"I gain it," he answered, "by going about
among the animals who are sick, and curing
them."

Then the elders said: "If that is so, teach us
your Power, and we will set you free; but if not,
you shall die."

T'hoo-chée-deh agreed, and they brought him
to town with honor.   For twelve days and twelve
nights he and the men stayed shut up in the *estufa;*
for two days fasting, and one day making the medicine-dance, and then fasting and then dancing
again, as our medicine-men do to this day.

On the last night, when he had taught the men
all the herbs and how to use them, and they had
become wise with practice, they sent T'hoo-chée-
deh out with a strong guard, that nothing should
harm him.   They set him down at the door of his
own house under the chapparo.   A law was made,
giving him full liberty of all that is grown in the
fields.   To this day, all True Believers honor him,
so that he is not called small any more.   When
they sing of him in the sacred places, they make

his house great, calling it *koor-óo-hlee naht-hóo*, the Mountain of the Chapparo. And him they call not T'hoo-chée-deh, the Field-Mouse, but *Pee-íd-deh p'ah-hláh-queer*, the Deer-by-the-River, that he may not seem of little honor.[1] For he was the Father of Medicine, and taught us how to cure the sick.

"*Tahb-kóon-ahm?*" cried the boys. "Is *that* why the Coyote always cries? And is that why we must never hurt the Field-Mouse, but show him respect, as to elders?"

"That is the very why," said Manuelito's grandfather, gravely; and all the old men nodded.

"And why—" began 'Tonio. But his father shook his head.

"*Tah!* It is enough. *Tóo-kwai!*"

So we stepped out into the night to our homes. And from the *Kú-mai*, black against the starry sky, the howl of Too-wháy-deh, wandering with his toothache, swelled across the sleeping village of the Tée-wahn.

[1] This is not an exception. Nearly all the animals known to the Tée-wahn have not only their common name, but a ceremonial and sacred one, which is used exclusively in the songs and rites.

XXXIII

A PUEBLO FAIRY TALE AND THE WAY IT WAS TOLD

ONE of Mark Twain's most amusing whims was to take a story of his own, turn it into French, and then translate it literally back to English. The result of transferring these strange idioms bodily was very grotesque, and a remarkable object-lesson as to the difference in "habits," so to speak, between two languages. This is one of the first things one notices in learning Latin — an inversion of the order of words in a sentence, which seems very awkward to us.

The Indian languages have not so many characteristic idioms; but the order of the sentence, and the fashion of compounding words, make an absolutely literal translation almost unintelligible. It may interest you to see exactly how one of these folk-stories is told — original Indian and all; so here is an interlined translation of such a story, each Indian word having printed under it the English word (or words) for which it stands.[1]

[1] In pronouncing the Tigua, *A* is like *ah*, and *U* like *oo* in "boo"; *I* and *ee* sound like *ee* in "deed"; *E* like *ay* in "day"; *Eh* like *e* in "bed"; *Ü* as in the German; *Hui* like "wee"—as which it is often spelled here; *Hue* like *we* in "wed"—also spelled here *weh*; (*n*) indicates that the vowel is to be pronounced "through the nose." The other letters have their ordinary English sounds. The apostrophe means a little holding of the breath after the consonant, before making the vowel sounds at all.

P'A-Í-SHIA

A TALE OF THE OLD

Nah-t'hú-ai kah-men-chú Tú-ai-f(n)ú-ni-hlú-hli
In a house,   they say,   Cane-Black-Old-Man

an   I-eh-bú-reh-kún-hli-o   I-eh-ch'ú-ri-ch'ah
and Ear-of-Corn-with-Husks-Woman, Corn-Yellow-Girl,[1] (and)

Na-chur-ú-chu   iṁ-u-u-f'hir   i-i-tú-ai.   Tú-ai-
Blue-Dawn(proper name) (and) their little son, lived they.   Cane-

f(n)ú-ni-hlú-hli   hlé-eh-chí-deh   t'ah-rá-da-kí-eh
Black-Old-Man   rain   worked for (to call).

I-eh-bú-reh-kún-hli-o   é-eh-wé   pú-nyu-páh.
Corn-Old-Woman   was   without eyes (blind).

Hú-bak Na-chur-ú-chu   tum-da-kín huib quí-eh-
Then   (proper name)   came at dawn whib-stick used

huí-mi-k'yé.   Hú-bak   I-eh-ch'ú-ri-ch'ah   ú-tir-
to run.   Then   Corn-Yellow-Girl   she used

k'yé.   Hú-bak   I-eh-bú-reh-kún-hli-o   be-ná
to grind.   Then   Ear-of-Corn-Old-Woman   she used

ú-u-nah-pi-en-nú-k'ye.   Nah-quai-yaí   ah-shi-
to the child take care of.   On the belt   she used

[1] N.'s sister.

16   241

yé-k'ye.   Jü-on-aí   ah-mí-bak   hu-e   Eh-beh-
to tie.   Far   when gone far, thought   she

aň bak   nah-quái   huü-shi-k'yé.   Hú-bak   shi-
thought,   the belt   she pulled back.   Then   (the)

hui-deh-báh   ah-ú-u   pú(n)-peh-cheh-a-bán.
eagle   the child   had eyed.

Hú-bak   t'á   huím-t'hu   t'á   shi-huí-deh   i-bán.
Then   one day   the eagle   came.

Hú-bak   ú-u   hlí-em-beh-bá.   Hú-bak   náh-quai-
Then   child   he stole.   Then   belt

huí-shi-ban.   Hú-bak   t'á   éh-u-u   shé-pah.   Hú-bak
she pulled.   Then   no child   tied.   Then to

I-eh-ch'ú-ri-ch'ah   tu(n)-am-bán ma-pé quú-huü-ri
Corn-Yellow-Girl   she spoke: " Hurry, come out;

jé-chu-ow-áh-chu   ín-u-u-mí.   Hú-bak   shim-ba
I don't know where   my little child."   Then   all

ki-eh-báht   u-shi-a-bán.   Hú-bak   p'ai-bá-na   eh
everywhere   asked they.   Then   nobody   had

shim-bé-bah.   Hú-bak   ki(n)-tú-aht   i-na-cá-cha
seen.   Then   pueblo   notice

hui-eh-bán.   Hú-bak   yú-a-huin-na   hué   em-mu-
given.   Then   nowhere   was   seen.

chéh-ba.   Hú-bak   hú-nak.   T'á   i-pí-eh-hue   bi-u-
Then   it was so on.   (Then) sorry   they

ban.   T'á   Tú-ai-f(n)ú-ni-hlú-hli   weh-eh   weh-hlé
were.   Then Cane-Black-Old-Man   did n't   rain

chi-t'a-rá-wa ta-kípa. Hú-bak t'á wéh-eh hlu-a-báh.
work for (by "medicine"). Then   did n't   rain.

T'á   hú-bak   shim-ba   eé-eh-ee   eh-teh-bán.
Then   all   corn   got dry.

Hú-bak   t'á   shim-ba   t'ai-nín   ee-hú-pi-o-bán.
Then   all   the people   hungry were.

Hú-bak t'á hú-wée-nu wée-wai Na-chur-ú-chu
Then   at last   again   (proper name)

wée-wai t'hum-dak-kín whib kui-eh-wee mee-wéh.
again   in the morning   (whib)   to run   went he.

Hú-bak yú-o-wáh mir-p'yén-ahp weh-náh-té-a-kem
Then   somewhere mesa in the middle day, inaccessible

nah-pán-ahp   shú(n)-mik   t'-rá-weh   u-ú-deh
it was,   passing by,   he heard   the child

ah-náh-ch'áh:
     singing:

> " *Chéh-e-máh-weh, máh-weh*[1]
> *Chéh-e-máh-weh, máh-weh*
> *tú-ti kéh-weh*
> *tú kéh-weh*
> *Sai-yah-di-keh*"

Hú-bak   hún   ta-rá-bak   bé-eh-win-ee-bán
Then   when   this he heard,   he   stopped

bé-eh-ta-wín-ee hím-ai.   Hú-bak   weé-wai   hú-
to listen   for.   Then   again   the

---

[1] Not Isleta words. Perhaps Chimayó. Many of the ceremonial songs are in other Indian languages — perhaps to add to the mystery with which the medicine-men surround their profession.

daht t'a-rá-ban.   Hú-bak ta tú(n)-weh pai-í-nah
same   heard he.   Then   said he: "No other:

wi'm-ah wé-eh-wéh nyú-deh in-chún-un-o-wé-i
         is n't   this   my nephew?
wem.
He is."

Hú-bak ta-mí-eh-weh wée-wai mah-kwi-wéh.
Then   went he   again   back.

Hú-bak tü-ai wám-bak.   T(n)-wéh men shi hui-deh-
Then   pueblo arrived he.   He said: "By the   eagle

báh in-chún-o-wé-i wé-eh-cheh-báhn. Hú-a-yú hún
my nephew   was carried.   That 's why so

té-aht'-ah-ra-báhn yu-áh wen-náht-t'hén-aht p'a-
I heard   where   he cannot,   and   no-

yín-a wéh-a-wan-hin-áht áh-na-pún.   Hú-bak-táh
body   can reach,   noise-making."   Then

u-béh-weh tum-dák wée-wai ah-mée-hee káh-bah
they told him: "To-morrow again   you go,   see

k'énd-ha hú-daht ah-t'áh-ra-hée. Hú-bak tü-bek
if   the same you will hear."   Then   next day

wée-wai mee-báhn. Nwe-bai-ee hú-daht wée-wai
again   he went.   True it was, the same   again

t'á-ra-báhn. Hú-bak tú(n)-wéh him-meh-én-chu
he heard.   Then   he said: "It is so;

yeh-deh eé-ku-wem.   Hú-bak ta ki(n)tú-aht
that   is he."   Then   the pueblo-in

ú-wan   ee-chái-beh-eh-báhn   ee-mee-héem-ai
the lads   were ordered   to go

ec-hlú-ch-wee-hím-ai bi-chu ee--méh-nah-t'héh-
to bring him down,   but   they could n't.
wah.

Hú-bak   hí-yo-kú-ak-kwó-a-bén   ee-chee-em-
Then   Stone-Layers[1]   flying
mée-ay.
were.

Hú-bak ee-bée-u-mée-way. Hí-yo-kú-ak-kwó-a-
Then   they   told them: "Bird-masons,

bén hée-ri-yú mah-whéh-mi bé-a-wa wai-kyé
       what   payment   want you   up there

u-ú-deh kú-ai-eé-ee ben-hlú--a-- wée-hée-mai?
child   lying there   to bring him   down ?"

Hú-bak yen-náh pee-eh-wée-am-báh. *Chee chee*
Then   they did n't   care.   (Their cry)
chee chee!

Hú-ni tu-mik kée-yeh-pu(n)ú-a-pu eé-hleu-
So   cried they   up and down   coming

mik ee-wér-ím-mik ée-t'ah-meé-ay. Hú-bak
down,   going up,   they were doing.   Then

wée-wai ee-beé-u- meé-way. T'a hu-wée nu
again,   again they spoke.   At last   one

17   [1] A kind of swallow. "Masons."

weém-ah tó(n)-wéh Ah, hée-a-men náh-pú(n).
(bird)   he said :   "Yes, there is some one talking."

Ta-hú-bak   ee-béh-t'a-win-nee-báhn.   Hú-bak
Then   listened   they.   Then

ee-u-béh-weh heér-ri-a ma-whéh-am-ee béh-a-
they told them :   "What   payment   want

wah bén-u-u hlú-a-wi him-ai.   Hú-bak eé-to'(n)-
you   our child   down   to bring ? "   Then   they

weh t'a-úm.   Hú-bak tai-ee-weé-rí-báhn bi-chu
said : "Piñones."   Then   up went   they,   but

ee-mén-naht-héh-wah.   Hú-bak ee-hlée-u-báhn,
they could n't.   Then   down came they,

eé-i-tú-meé-ay eé-meh-náh-teh-báhn.   Hú-bak
said they   then could n't.   Then

ta ee-béh-eh whém-beh-báhn.   Ta hú-bak ah-
they   were paid piñones.   Then   them-

wán-dah ee-tún-weh ah-chée-ee p'a-ü-ah-
selves   they said :   "To Grandmother-Spider-Old-

hlée-u ee-mée-heen.   Hú-bak ee-mée-báhn.
Woman   we will go."   Then   went they.

Hú-bak yú-o-áh ah-chée-ee p'a-ü-ah-hlée-u
Then   where   Grandmother-Spider-Old-Woman

tü-pán-aht ee-wam-bán.   Hú-bak ta eé-oo-
lived she   they arrived.   Then   said

mee-báhn hée-yah eé-nah-béhu-min-áp. Hú-bak
she :   "What   want you ? "   Then

eé-u-béh-weh.   Hú-in-kwee-nám.   Ah-bu u-ú-deh
they told her.   "So it is?   My poor   child

áh-nah-púm-nin.   Háh-ru máh-ku bé-y-kée téh
makes noise.   Wait,   grandsons,   wait me,   let

kar-chéh.   Ta-hú-bak ú-nah-kar-seh-wéh kü
us eat."   Then   her food she put up in acorn-

téh-u- ahu sa-chú-un kwée-a-ree-án.   Hú-bak
shells: mush,   atole-and.   Then

Hí-yo-kú-ak-kwó-a-bén hee-tú-weh Bah! áh-bu
the birds   said they: "Bah! Poor (us)!

pá(n)-yu h(n)-a-wáh- hee nú-din ow. Hú-nin máh
Who is it   will fill-in these shells?" "That-way-so, grand-

ku, ay-éh pee-eh   wéh-ki manhu-kár. Hú-bak to
sons, don't think.   Eat, yourselves."   Then

ee-tú(n) wéh há-wu ah-chée-ee   Him-eh-én
said   they: "Thanks, Grandmother.   Is that

chu heh-reé pán-yu hua-wáh-him-aí kim.
so,   and   who is it   will be filled?"   "You.

Hú-bak ee-mée-weh nah-hú-wah. Tú-kway-ee
Then   you go,   and you are filled." "Let us go

ka-báhn ee-mée-eh-chéh. Ta hú-bak eé-t'ú-a
to see   to go away."   Then   big

bú-ru kúr-ban. Hú-bak ta ee-mée-báhn yú-o
basket she took.   Then   they went   some-

áh meér-ahb   ú-wun in-nah- keé eé-pan-aht.
where on the mesa. The lads   waiting   were.

Hú-bak   u-ah-béh-wéh   in-chée-ee-wáy-ee   tahb
Then   they told her: "Our Grandmother,   will you

kéh-beh-yá-weh-weh   wai-keé-ay   u-ú-deh   kú-a-
dare   way up   child   ly-

yeé-ee   ben-hléhw-hée-ee.   A-áh   bi-chu   u-kém
ing   bring me down?"   "Yes,   but   take care

kée-ep   mah-wéh-eh-mu-hee.   Ta   wée-eh-ree-
up   not to look."   Then   she went

báhn.   Ta,   hee-táh   Ee-tü-ah-bú-   ru   chu-
up.   Then, "Here he is!"   The basket   she

mee-báhn.   Hú-bak   wai-mow-mú-ee   wai-keé-ee
hung down.   Then   look up there   way up

ah-chée-ee,   p'áh-nah-hleé-u   mah-mú-ee.
to Grandmother-Spider-Old-Woman   look up—they.

Hú-bak   ee-et'-ú-a-bú-ru   pú-ee-yéh-de-báhn.
Then   the basket   blew away.

In-dah   hún-ma'a-t'á-chi.   Éhr-eh.   In-dáh-a in-
"Do not do that."   She suffered.   "No,   my

chee-ee-wáy-ee   t'a   yan   kee-way-a-   mu-hee.
Grandmother,   now   we will not look up."

Wée-wai   t'ú-a-bú-ru   chu-mée-bahn   t'áú-a-hlú
Again   basket   she hung.   The baby brought

ee-báhn.   Hú-bak   bi-chu   shée-u-ú-deh   tin wéh-ai.
she down.   Then   but   eagle-young   only he was.

Ta   hú-bak   ee-wháy-bahn   tú-ai   tá-eé   wám-
Then   they carried to the pueblo   and   ar-

bahn. Ta in-náh-keen-wee-báhn hée-bah-kú
rived. Then tried they which way

eé-t'ai-peh- him ai wée-wai. Hú-bak sú-ah-
"people" could they make him again. Then the men

nin ee-ú-nah pee-in-ai. Hú-bak ta wee-énd-t'hu
the fathers of wisdom. Then for four days

ee-béhu-wa-yu-bún. Hú-bak wee-énd-t'hu-wáy-i
hungry went. Then in four days' end

nu-wid-deh-aí ee-t'ah-ra-tá-ban. Hun húyú-ai
in the night worked wisdom. So then

shée-u-ú-deh hláh-keh-báhn. Hú-bak ee-cháh-
eagle-child they set down. Then they

ta-báhn. Chú-pi nah-káh-wai A-mák-k'hür
sang. At the first words the Ma-koor hoop

dü-reh-báhn. Hú-bak kö-a-u ai-chin t'ai peh-
they rolled. Then to the neck down, "people" he

cheh-báhn. Wée-choo-wáy-ee máh-dür ai-kén ta.
became. The second to the waist down.

Pá-chu áh-way-eé kú-pee-a-khin. Wée-en-ai
Third time to the knees. Fourth

ee-eh-kó-ah-kweér-ai-chin. Pán-du-ai-kü-tim-báh.
to ankles down. Fifth perfectly (all over).

Hun hu-yú-ai. Ta ee p'áh klu-eh-mee-
So it finished. Then water they

báhn. Hú-bak p'ah-sú-a-beh-báhn to ehw-
warmed. Then water made him drink. He vom-

báhn   shim-ba   peé-run,   tú-whé-un,   pee-u-nín,
ited up   all the   snakes,   coyotes,   rabbits,

shee-chún   bai-ay-tee   shée-eh-wim-bah   hée-ree-áh
mice,   and vermin,   all   what

hée-ree-áh   náh-mee-kéh-wa-eh   ṣhée-wid-deh-báh.
all   was fed him   the eagle by.

Hun   hu-yu-   ai ta   im-mah   pee-wee-eh-cheh
So then about that time   he was   given over (to his

báhn.   Hú-bak   tá   eé-wheh-báhn   ún-tü-nai.
parents).   Then   they carried him   to their home.

Hú-bak   weé-wai   Tú-ai-f(n)ú-ni-hlú-hli   hlay-chid
Then   again   Cane-Black-Old-Man   rain

t'á-ra-ta-báhn.   Ta wée-wai   hlu-rid-deh   wéh-eh-
worked.   Again   rain   they

teh-báhn.   Ta náh-péh-ahw   ú-ee-eh-shám-bahn.
had.   On the fields   corn came up.

Ta   ú-káhp-páhn.   Hú-bak   ú-kö-wéh-wun.
It blossomed.   Then   it ripened.

Hún   hú-yu-   ai   ta   t'ai kah-bay-deh   áh-nah-
So   about that time people commander (Cacique) they

kah-cháh   wée-eh-cheh-báhn   eé-u   eé-eh-tu-   a
told   (to give leave),   corn   they were going

hím.   Hú-bak   ta   nah-tú(n)-kwin   pú-an   ee-u-
to pick.   Then   calling   they proclaimed   corn

eé-eh-tu-a.   Ta   t'ai-nin   eé-eh-tú-mee-báhn.
to pick.   Then the people corn went to pick.

Hú-bak eé-u kör-bahn hee-táh t'ai-kah-báy-deh-
Then   corn they brought into the   Cacique's

ai. Hú-bak u-púm-- pee-ay-báhn.   Hai-ku
house. Then   it they filled and more was left.   Go

nyú-din whay-eh-b'ai-kweer tü-u tu-wáh-weh-
these   to the east,   to the north; in the

eé-ahk mahw-whéh-wi.   Hú-bak nyú-din wheh-
(street)   take it.   Then   this   north-

u-weéw-kweer tú-now tu-wáh-weh-eé-uk mahu-
to-west,   west   the street   take up

whéhw-wi.   Hú-bak nyú-din whéh-en-ai-kweer
this.   Then   this   from west

tú-k'hu- tu-wáh-weh-eé-uk mahw-whéh-wi. Bá(n)
to south   in the street   take it.   And

yú-deh whéh-a-kwée-kweer,   tú-wáh-weh-eé-uk
this   from south to east   in the street

mahu-whéh-wi.
  take it.

  Hú-bak hún ee-béh-a-wak kee-tú-ai tah-báhn.
  Then   so   very glad   in the pueblo they lived.

  Tá-kee-whée-kay-ee.
    You have a tail on.

Now here is the story "made English." First
I did a Spanish version, and went over it several
times with the Indian narrator, who could understand Spanish and agreed that it was a good translation of the original. Then I tried it on other
Indians; and they all voted it "Kú-chu." I have
not tried to keep the metrical form, but tell the
story so that Americans will understand it in exactly the same sense that the Indian boys and girls
understood it when it was told them in the soft and
musical Tée-wahn.

Once upon a time, they say, Old-Man-with-a-
Black-Cane and his wife Ear-of-Corn-Woman
lived with their children — with their daughter
Yellow-Corn-Girl, and her baby, and their little
son Na-chur-ú-chu (whose name means Boy-of-the-
Blue-of-Dawn).

Old-Man-with-a-Black-Cane was the Rain-
Maker of the pueblo, and worked to bring the
rains. His wife was without eyes (blind). The
little boy Na-chur-ú-chu used to play *whib*[1] in the
morning. Then his sister Yellow-Corn-Girl used

[1] An ancient game in which the players race many miles, kicking a
small stick ahead of them. They must touch it only with their toes.
The aboriginal name of Isleta is Shee-eh-whib-bak — meaning "Knife-
shaped-Ridge-where-they-play-*whib*." The pueblo is built on a knife-
shaped reef of lava running across the ancient channel of the Rio Grande.

to grind corn on the metate. The old mother used to take care of the baby and to work, weaving a belt. She used to tie the baby at the end of the belt, so that he could play while she worked.

One day she thought about the belt and pulled it back, and there was no boy tied to it. An eagle had watched the child. That one day the eagle came and stole the child; and when his grandmother pulled the belt there was no child tied to it. Then she cried to her daughter, Yellow-Corn-Girl: "Hurry, come out! I don't know where our little child is." Then they began to ask about him from everybody all around. Nobody had seen him. Then notice (official heralding) was given throughout the pueblo to hunt for him; but nowhere could he be found, though they kept looking for him a long time. And all the people were sorry.

Then Old-Man-with-a-Black-Cane no longer worked to bring the rain. And there was no rain. And all the corn got dry. Then all the people were hungry. Then at last again Na-chur-ú-chu went out to play *whib* in the morning; and somewhere on a high mesa, in the middle of the day, as he passed by in his playing, he heard on this inaccessible cliff a child singing:

"*I am the grandson of Old-Black-Cane.*"[1]

When Na-chur-ú-chu heard this, he stopped and listened long. And again he heard the same song. And he said to himself: "Is n't this my nephew? Certainly it is."

[1] The rest of the verse is in an unknown language, and probably archaic.

Then he went running back to the pueblo; and when got there he said: "My nephew has been stolen away by the eagle! That's why I heard him crying, up where nobody can reach him."

Then they told him in the pueblo: "Go again to-morrow, and see if you hear the same." Then he went again next day. And it was true, for he heard the same thing again. And he said to himself: "It certainly is so, for that is my nephew."

And when he told it in the pueblo, the young men were ordered to go and bring the child down from the mesa; but they could not scale it.

The Stone-Layers (a kind of swallow)[1] were fly-ing all around; and the young men said to them: "Say, Birds, what do you want us to pay you to go up there and bring down the child that is lying there?" But the birds did n't pay any attention, and kept on flying and singing their song, crying up and down, as they sailed up and down:

"*Chee! chee! chee! chee!*"

Then the young men asked them again to help rescue the child; and at last one bird paid atten-tion and said: "There *is* some one talking." And all the birds listened.

Again the young men said to them: "What pay-ment do you want to bring our child down to us?"

And the birds said: "Piñon nuts."

"All right," said the young men.

---

[1] Stone-Layers—that is, masons; because these swallows build their nests of mud and pebbles on cliffs, under roofs, or in any sheltered place, in a fashion which makes one clan of the Pueblos believe they descended from the swallows and taught all the other Pueblos to be " Stone-Layers " and build adobe houses.

The birds went up and tried to bring down the
child; but they could not, and then they came back
and said they were unable. The young men paid
them their price in piñon nuts just the same.

Then the birds said: "We will gŏ to Old
Grandmother-Spider." And so they went, and
they came to where Old Grandmother-Spider
lived. She said: "What do you want?"

And they told her. And she said: "Is it so?
The poor child makes a noise. Wait, my grandsons, wait for me, let me eat first; and I want you
to eat with me."

So she made her dinner by putting out some
acorn-cups with mush and atole.

The birds said: "Mercy, poor us! Who will fill
these shells up for us?" But the Grandmother-
Spider said: "Grandsons, you should not think
that way. Eat, and fill yourselves."

"Thank you, Grandmother," they said; and they
ate, and they were filled. Then she took a big
basket of her own weaving, and they all went to
the mesa. The young men of the pueblo were
waiting. They said to her: "Grandmother, would
you dare go away up to where the child is lying,
and bring him down to us?" And the Spider-
Grandmother said: "Yes, but you must take care
not to look up at what I am doing." Then she
went up. "Here he is!" she cried; and she hung
the basket.

And they could not help it, but looked up to see
where the Grandmother-Spider and the basket
were; and when they looked up, the basket blew
away.

Then she called to them: "Grandsons, you must not do that;" and she was very sorry. So they said: "Grandmother, now we will not look up." So again she hung the basket, and brought down the boy.

But he was not a boy any more, but a young eagle—just a young eagle. So they carried this young eagle back to the pueblo, and tried what way they could make him a child again instead of an eagle. The Wise Old Men fasted for four days; and then after the four days' fast they worked in the night to change him back.

They set down the eagle-child among them, and they sang the first words of the sacred songs, and they rolled the sacred ma-koor hoop.

And when they sang the first words of the song and rolled the ma-koor hoop, the eagle-child became "like people" down to his neck. But the rest of him was like a young eagle.

Again they sang the song and rolled the hoop, and he became "like people" down to the waist. The third time they sang the song and rolled the hoop, and he was "like people" down to the knees; and with the fourth singing and rolling he was "like people" down to the ankles; and with the fifth he was a perfect boy again. And so it was finished.

Then the Wise Men warmed water, and made him drink it until he vomited; and he vomited up all the snakes, the coyotes, rabbits, mice, and other things which the eagle had fed him.

Then when he was restored to his natural shape, and purified, they carried him to the arms of his parents. Then once more Old-Man-with-a-Black-Cane began to work for rain; and the rain came down, and it came upon the fields; and the corn came up and blossomed, and then it ripened. So about that time the people came to the Cacique and told him they were ready to pick corn; and it was proclaimed that the corn should be picked; and the people went out and picked the corn and brought it out to the Cacique's house; and they filled his house up full, and more was left. They carried corn throughout the pueblo to the east, to the north, to the northwest, to the west, to the south, and all the other quarters of the compass, as he told them (giving enough to everybody).

And so they were all very glad in the pueblo, and lived happy, and had enough to eat.

You have a tail on you. (Now it 's *your* turn to tell a story.)